MAKING SENSE *of* US

MAKING SENSE OF US

An Essay on Human Meaning

∾

John Deakins

GRANVILLE ISLAND
PUBLISHING
GranvilleIslandPublishing.com

01 02 03 04 05 06 15 14 13 12 11

Library and Archives Canada Cataloguing in Publication
Deakins, John, 1934-
      Making sense of us : John Deakins.
ISBN 978-1-894694-76-6
      1. Self. 2. Individual differences. 3. Interpersonal relations.
I. Title.
BF697.D42 2010   155.2   C2010-907254-5

Editing by Tasha McCauley and Beatrice Dowd
Proofreading by Dawn-Louise McLeod and Adrianna W. Van Leeuwen
Indexing is by Bookmarks: editing and indexing
Book Design by Fiona Raven
Book Cover Photograph by Leanne Jijian Hume
Final Proof Reading by Neall Calvert
Electronic Prepress by Lawrence Boxall

Grateful acknowledgement is made to *New Directions Publishing Corporation* and *Carcanet Press Limited* for permission to quote the excerpt from "Asphodel, That Greeny Flower," from *Collected Poems 1939–1962, Vol 11.* Copyright 1944 by William Carlos Williams.

The text of this book is set in Minion Pro, a type designed in the U.S. in 1990 by Robert Slimbach.

Printed in Canada on recycled paper.

Granville Island Publishing
212 – 1656 Duranleau St.
Vancouver BC
Canada V6H 3S4
www.granvilleislandpublishing.com

This is for my children,
Sarah and Wendy,
and for all children, everywhere

Contents

Introduction   ix

1   Alfie: "What's it all about?"   1

2   Human Ambients   17

3   Belief   33

4   Survival, and Opportunity   45

5   Error   65

6   Optimizing Opportunity   85

7   Safeguarding Identity   91

8   Cooperation   111

9   Change   131

10   A Better Question—and an Answer   157

Commentary on the Notes   165

Notes   169

Bibliography   185

Acknowledgments   197

Index   199

About the Author   208

"Tut, tut, child," said the Duchess.
"Everything's got a moral if only you can find it."

—LEWIS CARROLL

Stil I wunt have no other track.

—RUSSELL HOBAN

Introduction

THIS BOOK IS ABOUT how we make sense: of ourselves, of one another, and of life. It is not about the particular kind of sense each of us makes, but rather about the manner in which we make it. Less, then, about what we have come to believe; more about how we have come to believe it.

At first, that sounds simple enough. There's a problem, though. To put it crudely, none of us can approach the question of how we make sense with a fully open mind. We have, all of us, become a part of something, and that something has become a part of us, before we have been able to start questioning what it is that we have become a part of. Indeed, that's as true for our species considered as a whole as it is for any single one of us. It's the sense we've already made that shapes the questions we're able to ask. We all start in the middle.

There's a further problem, too. Most of us are likely to feel pretty impatient with a whole book devoted to understanding how we construct what we believe. For the most part, we take our ability to make sense for granted; that is, until we discover that someone else's sense differs from ours, or someone else reveals that our sense doesn't make sense to them. Unfortunately, as a species, we have a pretty poor record of coming to terms with those differences, let alone resolving them. It's clear, in fact, that, together, we don't make very good sense at all. In continuously choosing to define one another in terms of our disagreements, we distract ourselves from truly encountering who we are. It's no wonder, then, that when we do manage to transcend immediate concerns long enough to concentrate on the largest questions, those questions, too, tend to be framed in ways that separate us both from one another and from ourselves.

I think it's important to declare at the outset, then, that I do not intend to avoid the largest questions. I do, however, intend to show that we're almost certainly not going to find better answers to those questions—let alone the more immediately pressing ones—until we can become much more aware of the implications of the assumptions we make in asking them.

If you can at least provisionally accept those statements, and also accept that every single one of us has an unavoidably different perspective on the reality we inhabit, can you and I—and indeed, ultimately, all human beings—nevertheless find some common ground upon which to share the dilemmas we face, and come to realistic grips with them?

Let's try this. We can, at least momentarily, step back from ourselves and endeavor to look at ourselves (that is, our individual selves, but also ourselves as a species) as if from the *outside*. This assumes that we can, at least in imagination, stand outside our experiences and appraise our own strange behavior. Unfortunately, however, this is hardly a whole answer, for not one of us can individually ever achieve total objectivity. What we can do is recognize that *together*, in the very process of sharing and comparison of multiple perspectives, we can approach it. We may not be able to stand completely outside ourselves, but others do, and together it may prove possible to avoid the worst kinds of subjective error.

It's more complicated than that, of course, but confronting those complexities is largely what this book is about. I very much regret that no book can have the character of a conversation in which there would be opportunity to engage fully in working through any inevitable differences in perspective. What a book can do, however, is provide a sufficient stimulus for those kinds of conversations to occur elsewhere, and that is what I profoundly hope for this one.

I'd like to start, then, with a statement that takes account of our inevitable differences of perspective, and yet sets them in our common context. I firmly believe that what is common to you and me both—indeed to all human beings—is that we all *try* to make the best sense we can. I trust that this is obvious enough to not require justification. Again, however, it's a bit more complicated than that.

All of us make the best kind of sense we *think* or *feel* we can.

The sense that other people make will often seem nonsensical to us, but since ours may seem similarly nonsensical to them, we must allow that the logic of others is as convincing to them as ours is to us. It is our failure to give weight to this one simple fact that has resulted in attempts throughout our history to "knock sense" into other people, that is, to knock *our* sense into them. Inevitably, such attempts have been doomed to failure, and all future attempts of the same ilk are likely to share a similar fate.

It isn't only aggressive attacks on our beliefs, however, that lead us to jump to their defense. Although all of us are to some degree attached to beliefs that only imperfectly represent the reality with which we have to deal, we do not easily relinquish those beliefs, even in the face of appeals to contrary evidence or carefully reasoned argument. Indeed, when it comes to trying to change the minds of others, it appears that no method of persuasion can lay claim to a record of infallible success. What are we to do? If someone else's sense is not as mine, and we are at loggerheads, how can it be discerned which of us is in error? If it is my opponent, what will be required to show convincingly that this is the case? If it is me, what will it take to convince me *I* am wrong? Further, what if we are both wrong?

These are the questions I intend to answer.

Fortunately, and without disregarding the unspeakably dreadful things we human beings have been able to justify doing to one another, I believe there are nevertheless grounds for our being at least cautiously optimistic. That may sound almost ridiculously naïve, but consider: because sense is *made*, and *by us*, the process of its making is available to our investigation, and therefore to our understanding and revision. The differences, antagonisms, and outright conflicts between human beings that arise because of our different experiences of life result from the working of processes that are common to us all. We can discover the logic driving those processes by looking at what is essentially similar in the way each of us transforms our individual experience of the world into a viable understanding of how best to act within it.

Since the kind of sense that human beings collectively make may be considered an expression of where we are in our evolution, and further, an aspect of where Nature is in its own evolution, a major thread throughout the book is my effort to see all our current problems and cumulative achievements in the context of the whole evolutionary thrust of Nature itself. This perspective, I hope, conveys an invitation not only to a greater humility about our place in the great everything, but also to a sense of awe and wonder at the potential of which we are a part.

It is for this reason that the book begins not with us but rather with the very character of life. How the present surviving forms of life can be thought to make sense manifests in the obvious fact that all those life forms are not only pursuing their own immediate purposes, but are also, over their evolutionary history, contributing to some transcendent realization that is subjectively unknowable to any individual within its own life span. The early forms of life can have had no ability to envisage their role in the evolution of trees, flowers, privet hedges, mice, men, pigs, alligators, eagles or chickens, let alone in the evolution of an intelligence capable of contemplating its own evolution, and, indeed, that of everything else.

For our purposes, I shall not be focusing on the actual transition from inorganic to organic forms (that is, with the very beginnings of life). However, if we can succeed in our task of better understanding how we ourselves make sense, we may well find that we are not only better placed to deal with the implications of that enormous shift in the character of existence, but also (dare I say it?) with the possibility (or perhaps probability) of similar shifts in the future, and also the likelihood that we ourselves might have a significant part to play in them.

In pursuing our immediate task, then, I'm suggesting that we'd do a better job of understanding ourselves if we could discern not only how we as a species have come to differ from all other forms of life, but also in what ways we remain similar to them. Paying closer attention to the characteristics we share with other forms of life will hopefully enable us to slough off at least some of our arrogance. Paying closer attention to the ways we are profoundly different from those other forms will arguably permit a more subtle understanding of ourselves. I hope you will agree that we badly need both.

As you move through the book, you may find some of the concepts used unfamiliar, but I trust that, in testing their validity against your own experience, you will come to find them indispensable. I am presuming, too, that you already share my belief that what we are about is a more than trivial enterprise. The issues I try to confront in this book—and those I believe you yourselves will confront in reading it—are in microcosm the issues confronting humankind. Given that our very survival as a species might well depend on finding a way to make better sense together than we currently do, we're unlikely to find a more significant task.

I don't think we've consciously distracted ourselves from that task in the past. It's rather that we have, over the course of our history, given considerably more time and attention to making *our own different kinds of sense* than we have to questioning how it has come about that we do so, or how indeed it is that we make any kind of sense at all. Even if our survival as a species were not currently at risk, the latter enterprise would both deserve and require more respect than we usually give it. For the most part, we tend rather to get caught up in the hurly-burly of living, and hurriedly make the best accommodations we can to the incongruities we face.

It has to be said, however, that the circumstantial factors affecting our ability to accommodate to incongruity may differ profoundly. The freedom to act in a refugee camp is not commensurate with the freedom to act in an affluent democracy. Agonizing over whether or not to sell one's child into sexual slavery is not at all commensurable with the kinds of choices likely to be faced by any of us in a position to read this book. Gross inequality of opportunity for choice is a brutal fact of our present world, and that includes any individual's chances of making better sense of it. For those scarcely able to survive amidst the horrors of tribal, civil, or ethnic conflict, or in the aftermath of devastating natural disaster, more immediate concerns have irrefutable priority. It is nevertheless clear that almost universally—and notwithstanding the fact of inequalities between us—the demands of day-to-day living do not seem to allow us time for fundamental questioning. As one author puts it, such contemplation is hard to sustain—even for those of us in a position to do so—because it always seems to be off the subject.[1]

My commitment in this book is instead to show (as indeed that author, Kenneth Burke, does himself) that our manner of making sense is the fundamental subject, for it determines the shape of everything that we have come to believe, and therefore, in any circumstance, of everything we choose to do. It is the way we make sense that both determines and defines who we are able to be.

My purpose, however, reaches further. If we can come to

understand better *how* we make sense, I believe we'll not only be able to make better sense of who we are and what we are about, but also—collectively and over time—better sense of our place in existence itself. I hope, then, not only that you already share this belief or that I can successfully justify it to you, but also that what you read in the following pages will suggest ways in which all of us can play a part in fulfilling the promise it contains.

Am I likely to achieve my purpose? Indeed, in reading this book, are you likely to achieve yours? Perhaps the answers to both questions simply depend on our recognizing that in this book, as in life itself, we are involved in what is essentially a joint enterprise. Undoubtedly you are right to expect a great deal from me; my title justifies such an expectation. What may not be as apparent is that I am similarly expecting a great deal from you.

Given that my part of the job in relation to this book is largely done, and yours is just beginning, what can I say here that will be of most help to you? My principal concern is that you be consciously prepared for the difficulty that all of us have to confront if we are truly to achieve a better understanding both of one another and of ourselves.

I'll be blunt: however desirable it might be, and fellow humans as we are, none of us can actually walk a mile—or indeed any distance—in another person's shoes. Each of our lives is different from that of any other's. In relation to this book and our joint participation in it, then, I cannot possibly have found exactly the right words, or the right metaphors, or the best examples, to persuade you of the validity of what I say. I cannot walk in your shoes; you cannot walk in mine. What I do ask of you, at least for the short distance of this book, is that you endeavor to walk at my side. The path I take won't always be obvious to you, nor indeed its direction. Preoccupied with finding my way, I was myself not fully aware of where it would lead. I am acutely aware, however, that it is *you* I must rely upon to set your own pace, stopping when you need to draw breath or ponder, as you undoubtedly will, the meaning of what you have read.

Whatever doubts you have, whatever kind of sense each of you individually makes of what I say, I nevertheless believe that in committing to walk with me, you will be honoring both yourself and our fellowship as human beings. I also believe that we will be further on our way to honoring those whose opportunity for choice in their lives is at present only a minute fraction of that which is available to us. Who knows? Together, we may be able to change the world.

Alfie: "What's it all about?"

BEGINNING WITH THE hardest question of all may seem almost perverse, but whether we like it or not, it's the question that bears on everything else we do in our efforts to make more immediate sense of our lives. It is probably, in fact, the largest common question we are able to ask.

Do we really expect to be able to answer the question? Well, we've certainly persisted in the search for an answer for much of our known history, and we have repeatedly demonstrated our ability to contrive a variety of answers. The sheer number of differing religious beliefs—past and present—testifies both to the intensity of our search and to the urgency of our desire to find. Of course, there is also an alternative to trying to find, imagine, or even speculate about the nature of the answer: one simply accepts that the question cannot be answered, and thus is essentially meaningless as far as any relevance to our own lives is concerned. In that case, what we may devise in consequence is a purely subjective purpose for our own existence. After all, if we cannot discern an overall design, then each one of us can find ample justification for becoming one's own designer. The resulting range of subjectively justified purposes is probably almost as large as humankind itself, and is in consequence scarcely likely to be of value to anyone attempting to face the larger question.

So we do the best we can—or, at least, we do the best we think we can—and each of us in our own way gets on with living. For many of us, indeed, our day-to-day preoccupations seem to leave little room for anything else.

The largest questions are nevertheless hard to get away from; every piece of sense we make is set in their overwhelming context. We may individually, and even in concert, effectively engage with a series of more circumscribed questions, and as our scientific discoveries cumulatively show, we have a pretty good record over millennia of coming to a better understanding of the purely physical aspects of the working of the universe. On the metaphysical aspects, however, our efforts have been less successful. In the silence of a lonely room, each of us is probably still agonizingly unsure of what it's all about. What is it all for? More to the immediate point, what are *we* for?

Unfortunately, dwelling on the sheer size of such questions at the very outset can stop us dead in our tracks. It doesn't do them justice, however, to yield too readily to their apparent unanswerability. Let's stage a temporary strategic retreat, then, and try to find an easier approach. The largest questions will still be around when we are better prepared for them.

Let us begin where we can at least gain a foothold. Happily, the very form of Alfie's question gives us just the kind of crevice we need.[1] Since the form of any question necessarily predetermines the form of all its possible answers, it also determines the very nature of those answers. If one asks a friend what he or she is going to do tonight, we know that we are not going to receive the answer, "It is blue." Such an answer belongs to a different sort of question. What, then, is the kind of answer that the form of Alfie's question requires? What assumptions are we making about the nature of that answer? Further, what kinds of answers does the very form of the question *prohibit*?

In arguably its most frequently encountered form—that is, the form in which Alfie posed it—the question presumes that the answer will reveal some kind of *purpose*. Any kind of answer that excludes the presumption of purpose is thus prohibited.

How has it come about that we choose to ask the question in that particular way?

Our assuming that some universal purpose must be the fundamental determining factor in existence most probably stems from our experience that intent is irrefutably characteristic of our own lives. Each of us is defined in large part by what we want and what, in consequence, we are prepared to do. Indeed, every form of life seems to be permeated with motive. It is the presence of motive, in fact, that we traditionally use as the criterion for distinguishing what is alive from what is not. The view that all matter, whatever its form, ultimately tends towards disorganization and decay[2] heightens and strengthens our sense that there must be something very special in the apparently contrary tendency for Nature to evolve ever more complex forms of motivated organization. In our experience of our own planet, life seems to seize even the slenderest of opportunities to establish its presence. Nettles, grasses, lupins, and foxgloves quickly colonized the bombed sites of my childhood.

Unfortunately, the very nature of human language directs our thinking towards the apparent discontinuity between what is alive and what isn't. The connectedness between those two modes of being is nevertheless a plain fact of our existence. Our task here, then, is not so much to establish that connectedness; it is to take on the mystery of our own particular being in a somewhat different way than we have hitherto. Although we tend intuitively to accept the existence of motive in ourselves as a given, we can also examine it more carefully than we are wont to do, and take more time to ask the questions which place us more clearly in the overall context of existence itself. Obviously we are most immediately concerned about purpose in our own lives. If we can step back for a moment from our immediate personal concerns, however, and see them in the light of their larger context, a far more encompassing question presents itself: what can we deduce about the part played by individually pursued purpose in the evolution of the universe itself? More, what potentially is humanity's role in the answer to that question?

These are not only hard questions to answer; they are hard questions to ask. The existence of purposeful life seems totally at odds with our widely believed assumption that the universe is evolving mechanically according to apparently inexorable physical laws.[3] Our very presence, then, presents a conundrum for us. It is not surprising that in consequence so many of us should intuitively postulate a designer who set the whole thing in motion in the first place. The existence of purpose is hard for us to comprehend without at the same time conceiving the existence of an agent. The very asserting of the existence of a supreme agent, regardless of the multiplicity of forms that assertion may take, can thus itself be considered a kind of intuitive extrapolation from what we experience as a given in our own lives.

Many years ago, when my daughters were in their very early years, I can remember feeling flummoxed by something my younger daughter had done, and almost without thinking asked her "Why did you do that?" She looked at me in genuine bewilderment and said, as if it were the most obvious thing in the world, "Because I wanted to."

Let's look a bit more carefully at the assumptions implicit in the idea of agency, and of agents.

It is generally accepted, I believe—and indeed intuitively self evident—that from the dawn of life itself, living beings have distinguished themselves from inorganic matter by being able to relate to their surroundings. This engagement may be purely responsive, or re-active, in that the organism simply identifies those aspects of the environment that are important to it, and then responds to those circumstances in the ways that best serve its purpose. In short, it adapts. The engagement may also, however, be at the organism's own initiative, as when it deliberately seeks out those aspects of the environment that are useful to it. In many animal forms, indeed, the organism may actually modify the environment to enhance its usefulness. Even termites build castles. We are quite justified, I think, then, in defining life as matter which has not only organized itself, but also organized itself around some motivating purpose. The strength of our intuitive supposition is nicely portrayed in the very way we discuss the matter: organisms are, by definition, *organized*. It is thus a feature of our conceptualization itself that we recognize organization as simply the formal evidence of the existence of motive.

Can we be more specific? Of what does organic motive consist?

So far as we can discern, the activity of every genus of living being (including ourselves) appears to be directed towards living, creating offspring, and thus assuring the survival of its kind.

Each of these motives is characteristic of the essential process in which all life forms are engaged. That process necessarily depends on the circumstances in which any life form finds itself, circumstances that include both the presence and the activity of other life forms, all of which are similarly engaged in achieving their own survival. All are in the process of *becoming* (as indeed are we). The resulting development of increasingly adaptable and versatile forms has thus far been a dominant feature of all life on Earth, just as has the extinction of those forms whose ability to adapt proved insufficient. In the absence of more extensive evidence than is available to us at the moment, it would be difficult to persuade ourselves that any life form—wherever it might exist in our universe—could be characterized otherwise.

Although we may consider the ability to register the state of the surrounding world and to act upon it as an essential feature of all life, there is nevertheless a gradation of ability. The simplest unicellular organisms have only a minimal range of perceptual and action ability; the more complex organisms of both plant and animal life have powers of perception, and action (and thus of adaptability) that inspire wonder in even the most experienced of observers. Richard Dawkins' book, *Climbing Mount Improbable*, presents an awesome sampling of some of the most remarkable of these. I still get shivers down my spine when recalling the hair-raising story of how the fig plant managed to contrive its survival.

Even with such vast variation from simple to complex, however, the essential form of abilities appears to be similar in all life forms subject to Darwinian evolutionary processes. In each individual life span, all take some form of notice of what is happening around them; all in some way register what they have noticed; all then do something about it. In sum there is:

a perceiving function,

a processing function (which may include "thinking" and deciding), and

an action function.

In more complex life forms, the physical systems required for these functions are the sense organs (which differ, of course, from species to species), a controlling nervous system (likewise), and the effector apparatus (i.e., those parts of the creature that it uses to *do* anything).

In some forms of life, however, where the simplicity of the organic structure does not require the complexity of a central nervous system, it isn't really possible to discern a thinking function, since the perceptions and actions of the creature or plant may simply be characterized as tropisms (the sun-tracking ability of the sunflower, for example) or reflexes (as in the closing of the Venus flytrap). The perceptual and action functions of these contemporary life forms may thus be thought of as basic physiological givens, but it's probably more useful to think of them as simply current expressions of where that particular form is in its own evolution. We may nevertheless treat these perceptual and action abilities as metaphorically containing the autonomic defining "assumptions" that together specify what each creature actually *is*. This is not to imply that there is any reasoning process on the part of such creatures. On the other hand, we must be careful lest we characterize those creatures as being machine-like, or (as current jargon might have it) "hard-wired." Both such summaries would deny them the possibility of any evolutionary trajectory. Clearly, we need to be careful with our metaphors. The manner in which metaphors can be used and misused will deserve our closer attention later.

For human beings it is perhaps humbling to realize that, within our own bodies, the autonomic subsidiary systems which control and regulate the basic physical processes upon which our lives depend are not only utterly beyond our conscious control, but can be found functioning similarly in the most primitive life forms known to us. Without these processes, *we* would not survive. Even in the face of that knowledge, however, I don't think many of us would be willing to sum ourselves up as being pre-programmed bits of machinery. The machinery metaphor directs our attention towards a kind of historical static "givenness," and away from awareness of the continuously evolving *process* of which all of us are a part.

In every animal, the assumptions of its subsidiary systems are an essential aspect of its being, although as we shall argue later, the fact of being a living entity is not itself synonymous with a conscious awareness of identity. To be aware of oneself *as a self* requires a different mode of being-in-the-world.

Self-aware or not, however, any organic entity subject to competitive survival processes is physically separated from its surroundings by its boundary layer. This edge between inside and outside, self and not-self, is also the means of exchange between each organism and its surroundings. It thus constitutes not only the means of entry for nourishment and the evacuation of wastes, but also the means for perception of what is self, and what is not. When we painfully stub a toe, there's little doubt about where our personal physical boundary is.

The nature of the boundary layer, however, varies enormously across species, so that what is inside and what is outside can have an utterly different meaning than the one we are familiar with in our own case. In some species, only particular classes of individuals have functions that in other species every individual has, so that in some species it is the total social colony that appears to function as a single entity. Termites, for example, have such functions so specialized that "warrior" termites in some species are unable to feed themselves, and must be tended to by "caregiver" or "worker" forms. Each of these forms is anatomically *dissimilar*.

It seems a long way from plant to animal life, although biologists tell us that it is sometimes difficult to decide whether a given life form should be assigned to the plant or to the animal kingdom, or—hedging one's bets—to both. If, however, we set aside formal categories and concern ourselves rather with life *processes*, many differences of form seem less significant. As Kevin Lynch points out, "A plant appears unconscious to us, but if we speed up its movements by time-lapse photography, the plant seems to become a perceiving, reacting animal."[4]

For the moment, then, let's keep our attention firmly on the processes common to both plants and animals. The simplest way for us to understand any life form's relationship to its environment is by discerning whether that plant or creature registers its surroundings as unfavorable or noxious (and therefore to be avoided or defended against in some way), neutral (and therefore to be disregarded), or favorable (and therefore to be engaged with).

Again, in the simpler organic forms, it is unlikely that there is any actual discrimination of irrelevant circumstances or events. Such organisms avoid noxious conditions in much the same way as they respond to positive environmental circumstances: that is, reflexively, and it is only the specifically noxious or favorable which trigger a response.

Clearly, too, the range of responses available to a living entity in the face of variation in the environment differs enormously across species, in much the same manner as the perceptual range does. Obviously, the range of activity available to animals is more extensive than that available to plants, although both animals and plants can be shown to have evolved marvelously versatile protective and adaptive behaviors within their specific limits.[5] Plants, of course, survive and procreate without any motor functions whatsoever. Trees may not be able to run away from fires, but many have developed ways to survive them. Some species of trees have, over generations, actually come to depend on fire to create the conditions in which their seeds can germinate.

Regardless of an individual creature's repertoire of perceptual abilities, however, the apparent ability to discriminate dangerous from favorable must be considered an absolute necessity for every life form. Just as fundamental, too, is the weighting of protective responses over engagement ones. Even creatures without central nervous systems can be shown to have quicker protective responses than engagement responses.[6] The dominant concern of reflex action is the protection of the organism. In the case of communal organisms, this might even involve the sacrifice of individuals to protect communal existence.[7]

Being preferentially alert to danger, however, is only one part of the story. Protection for survival is simply a necessary precondition for any organism to engage in life as fully as its nature permits.

When it comes to considering the functioning of animals, the "higher" animals (and particularly human beings), it may be thought that these three categories of discrimination are crude, and characterize only inadequately the more subtle discriminations (we might even say "judgments") made routinely by these more actively versatile forms. However, it seems unarguable that in regard to direct sense experience of the world, these fundamental discriminations remain the most *important* discriminations, as the physical survival of all creatures depends on them. In one major respect, we human beings may be considered an exception to this general rule. I shall argue that that exception itself epitomizes the major challenge our species currently faces. We'll get to it shortly.

Regardless, however, of the complexity of the perceptual and action repertoires of a creature, it is important to emphasize that the repertoire is a *given* for each creature on the basis of its existing physiological apparatus. It is given, that is, for each creature inside the bubble of its own life. It may be that the power of a species to respond over generations to change in its environment is enhanced by the ability of apparently dormant genes to answer new demands, or genetic mutations to transcend prior adaptive limitations. In some species, indeed, the rapid rate of reproduction across generations is an important factor in their survival and development. (Modern bacteriologists, as well as the medical staff of our hospitals, are particularly well-placed to note the speedy adaptive responses of bacterial strains to successive antibiotic agents.) Nevertheless, as the extinction of numberless species bears witness, it must be recognized that there is a threshold beyond which—even across many generations—adaptation is not possible. In the span of an individual life, by contrast, for all creatures except the human animal, adaptability is determined by the limits of the creature's existing perceptual and effector abilities, whether autonomic or willed, conscious or unconscious.

In relation to the simplest organisms, however, it is clearly inappropriate to speak of consciousness, or even of volition. For example, in some animals, the same organic substance may have both perceptual and motor functions. It is thus the whole animal that registers, engages with, or withdraws from the environment it has registered. The whole animal, in fact, functions as an automaton.[8]

In more complex organisms, where the perceptual and action functions have resulted in differentiated organs, and the range and complexity of those functions require the coordinating function of what we have come to call a "central" nervous system, we are more justified in postulating a consciousness—albeit a circumscribed one—since the weighing of choices is clearly a factor in the internal processes of such animals. The purpose of the receptor organs, central nervous systems, and effector organs in such animals can then be thought of as enabling each controlling organism to make the best of its environmental opportunities, or in some cases, to create them.[9] With regard to these more complex forms, (of which we ourselves are obvious exemplars) let us attempt a general statement that, although necessarily made at a purely abstract level, nevertheless omits nothing essential to our understanding of them. The coordinating, thinking function of any animal's central nervous system consists of

– making the best kind of "sense" it can out of what it is able to perceive, both about the external world and about its own internal state, some of which will be processed without awareness;

– "choosing" the best of a range of possibilities for action; coordinating action; and

– appraising the results through special attention to data from the receptor organs, including data about the internal state of the organism.

It's unfortunate that such a generalized description of animal sensibility is unable to convey the wonder we might experience at witnessing those functions in action. Indeed, it is unfortunate that discerning, abstracting, and analyzing the principles at work in any experience of the world risks rendering that experience almost bloodless. Standing back in order to understand a process is one thing. Being fully alive in any given moment is quite another. Let's eschew analysis for a moment, then, and recall something of the wonder of being fully alive. Most of us can probably recall occasions when we have experienced that wonder. One of my own most valued memories is of encountering a large group of Pacific white-sided dolphins in western Canada's Desolation Sound, off the mainland coast of British Columbia. The dolphins, who were traveling south, immediately seized upon the opportunity presented by their chance encounter with our small open motorboat to surf inside the boat's bow wave, race inside the turbulence of its propeller wake, and subsequently, in coordinated groups, to perform those astounding and dramatic jumps so beloved of nature program watchers everywhere. We and the dolphins actually played together for some twenty minutes or so, until breaking off from us, the dolphins resumed their journey south, porpoising in unison until they were out of sight. The dolphins returned to their own business, and we—perhaps somewhat more reluctantly—returned to ours.

I'm similarly reluctant to return to my abstract summary of the way the processes involved in such events can be analyzed in terms of the principles they illustrate (I'm still entranced at re-living my memory), so perhaps I should simply leave you a moment to ruminate further on my memory, or perhaps one of your own—for assuredly you must have similar memories. It bears saying, however, that such vivid memories are good reminders that the processes we are endeavoring to understand are neither as mechanistic nor as linear as the clumsiness of the representational system of language unfortunately tends to render them.[10] Both the clumsiness of language and its miraculous versatility will occupy our attention a little later.

Meanwhile, let's attempt a summary: any central nervous system enables a creature to make the best sense of the world that it can, in order for the organism to function "sensibly" within it; that is, to achieve the optimal circumstances for it to survive, to live, to procreate, and thus unknowingly over generations to realize as fully as possible the potential of its nature. These purposes, summed, as it were, throughout Nature, can logically be seen as subsidiaries of the overarching process through which Nature is realizing itself; that is, accomplishing its own realization. Nature "naturing," as Spinoza called it.

Again, it is difficult to talk about this process without finding oneself inferring some final predetermining purpose. Most notably, we have to be particularly alert to our tendency to anthropomorphize Nature itself into something like a divine mother, as many of our ancestors did. In order to continue avoiding any such human-centered inference, let us endeavor to hold as consistently as possible to our awareness that our current knowledge restricts us to only a partial understanding of the process of which we are ourselves a part. In our own bodies, the red blood corpuscles have no awareness of their importance to the body that contains them, nor do the white corpuscles "know" that they are essential to the protection of the whole organism. In the great scheme of things, all entities may have a status and a function in relation to larger entities of which they have no ken. Our own awareness of ourselves as a part of something much larger is still not widespread. James Lovelock's most recent book, *The Vanishing Face of Gaia,* clarifies the extent to which that very ignorance has contributed to the global crisis we are still struggling to confront.

Notwithstanding the limits of our understanding, however, I think it's justifiable to assert that for any creature, the most powerful means of making sense and subsequently acting upon it, is for that organism to have three reciprocally coordinated systems:

– A receptor system that can discriminate extensively and accurately. (Those dolphins were as aware of us as living beings as we were of them, and almost certainly more aware than were we of the possibilities for play made available by a fortuitous encounter with a particular kind of fast-moving marine object.)

– A central nervous system that can store and retrieve the most detailed memories of prior events and outcomes, identify the recurring patterns in such data, and organize them into systematic and transferable understandings, thus enabling it to extrapolate from past experiences to current circumstances. (The dolphins clearly knew from past experience that playing with motorboats was something they enjoyed.)

 – An effector system with the widest range of possibilities for action. (Jumping in unison groups? No problem!)

These parameters also need to come with a rather severe set of caveats.

 – If a life form has insufficient (or insufficiently sensitive) sense receptors to register a particular feature or event in its environment, then that particular feature or event can be deemed not to exist for that life form (at least, as a factor in its awareness, and therefore in its choosing how to act).

 – Similarly, the range of action available to an organism for adaptive or creative purposes is necessarily limited to what its effector apparatus is capable of. Pigs cannot fly.

 – The characteristics of the action apparatus available to the organism not only determine what it can do, but how it registers its world.

In brief, each distinct organic form lives in a different, unique, subjectively experienced world. Think, for example, of the turkey vultures or the recently released surviving California condors soaring high over the mile-deep Grand Canyon, and the meaning to them of three-dimensional space and distance. Think of the sea mammals, like those dolphins, who live in a weightless deep space, and communicate with one another by transmitting vibrations through a medium in which sound travels three times faster than it does in air, and where the range of visibility is so much more restricted than it is for land-dwelling creatures. Think of those more recently discovered organisms which live and flourish in the extreme temperature of deep-sea volcanic vents, and so on, for creature after creature and every conceivable habitat, until the edge of our knowledge is reached, and the power of our imagination exhausted.

That each species is unique, however, should not preclude us from enquiring more deeply into the common character of the worlds occupied by all creatures. We may well find that investigating what is common to both ourselves and other creatures will permit us to discover elements of our own situation from which our subjective concerns have distracted us.

The pioneering work in this area was carried out in the early years of the twentieth century by the brilliant biologist Jakob Von Uexküll.[11] He suggested in 1926 that the unique experienced world of any life form can be mostly fully understood by exhaustively investigating the two defining aspects of its aliveness.

The first of these consists of the activity of an organism's *inner* perceiving, thinking, and action abilities. This aspect Von Uexküll called the "inner world." He saw it as serving two somewhat different functions: on the one hand, monitoring and managing the internal processes necessary for the creature to sustain its life, and, on the other, registering and responding to the circumstances in its environment having relevance to its survival.

It is important to note, then, that in all creatures—even the most advanced[12]—the general internal maintenance tasks are carried out automatically, without a conscious weighing-up of what to do. Such tasks nevertheless also require perception, choice, and action. In our own case, examples of such tasks are heartbeat, digestion, and temperature control. All the sense that is made in such cases is out of our awareness, and thus independent of our conscious will. It is this kind of combinatorial organizing ability that defines what is inside and what is outside, and thus makes any creature (or in some species, a whole colony) a functioning entity, rather than a collection of bits. In short, it is what makes any creature what it is.[13]

The second aspect of aliveness Von Uexküll called the entity's "outer world," a concept that is perhaps best understood as the total potential world accessible to the creature's senses and within the compass of its ability to act. A creature's outer world, it should be emphasized, is *not* identical to its environment, since there may be many aspects of an animal's environment that cannot be registered by its sense organs and are not subject to its ability to act. In the English translation of Von Uexküll's work, outer world is usually rendered as "ambient world" or simply "ambient." Since there is already a body of work in English that has accepted this usage, I shall do so also.

The conscious activity of any animal is of course concerned with managing the creature's interaction with its ambient world. The outcome of this activity is nevertheless dependent on circumstance. Any particular circumstance may exceed the ability of particular individuals to adapt to it, but it may also overwhelm the adaptive power of the species itself. In the short and the long run, then, both the survival of a species and its potential for development are subject to the power of the challenge offered to it by the rest of Nature. The organism may propose, but it is the rest of Nature that disposes.[14]

Is our own situation in Nature any different?

2

Human Ambients

JUST AS IT IS intuitively evident to us that all organisms are imbued with motive, so too does it seem pretty obvious that our human motives are extraordinarily different from the motives of other life forms. What is the nature of this difference? In the most fundamental respects, we may indeed be characterized exactly as other life forms are. We *are* animals, and, as such, our ability to engage with the world *is* totally described by the range, versatility, and power of our perceptual, processing, and action abilities.

It is immediately apparent, however, as we move from this generalization to a specific and detailed analysis of our human world, that we, unlike other life forms, have been able to transcend the naturally given physiological limits of our perceptual and action abilities. In consequence, the size of the human ambient world is significantly larger than our simple physiological capabilities would suggest. Indeed, the *potential* extent of our ambient world, if not without ultimate limit, is certainly beyond our current ability to determine.

There are many examples of our ability to transcend the naturally given apparent boundaries of what we can perceive and how we can act. In the arena of sense perception, for example, our natural visual ambient range is inferior in some respects to those of some other animals. We cannot see as acutely as eagles, for example, nor into the infrared part of the spectrum, as chickens can.[1] Yet human beings have been able to devise adjunct instruments that have permitted us to transcend the perceptual abilities of both. Our telescopes can probe far out into the darkness of the universe, our microscopes and other instruments into the very structure of matter itself; we can detect the presence of otherwise invisible objects by echo-location; we can hear orchestras half a world away; we can listen to radio-transmissions from Mars.[2]

The same kind of enhancement is true for our action abilities. We cannot fly like birds, nor swim like fish, but we have been able to devise and manufacture artifacts enabling us to approximate such abilities. We can't exactly swim like fish, nor fly like birds, but we can get close. If, too, we suddenly discovered that there was some aspect of piggy perception or activity that was useful for us to emulate, there is little doubt but that we could do so.

What is it that has so successfully enabled us to reach out beyond our physiologically given limits? The answer lies in the extraordinary nature of our internal handling of the data we receive from our senses. We have, in fact, an ability that is so familiar to us that we are almost oblivious of its presence:

The world we have constituted for ourselves is comprised not only of the physical artifacts we have designed and developed to expand our ambient, but also, and more fundamentally, of the abstract mental representations that have enabled us to do so.

Possibly we are less attentive to the manner in which our mental processes function because we've simply been too busy putting them to practical use. Yet it is not only the devising and manufacture of our physical artifacts that have required our attention, nor even what we've needed to do in order to use and maintain them. It is also the vastly enlarged possibilities for action that they have permitted. Just a short sample list should be an adequate reminder of the range of our inventiveness: we have microscopes; binoculars; telescopes. We have cameras, television, radios, reproductive audio equipment, computers and telecommunications. We have bicycles, cars, airplanes, rockets, ships, submarines, and scuba gear. We have wheelchairs, protective clothing, and lamps. We've developed drugs to compensate for internal chemical deficiencies; we have surgical procedures to prolong or enhance the quality of life. We have prosthetics that can compensate for the loss of limbs or particular body function. In sum, we have been—and continue to be—very busy indeed.

All of these developments, both physical and procedural, can be considered as contrivances, or *synthetic extensions* of the physiologically given "natural" ambient of human beings. As the designer David Pye observed, "The man-made world, our environment, is a work of art, all of it, every bit of it. But not all good."[3]

In addition to our specifically physical instrumental activity, however, we also have vast resources for the expression of purely mental activity. We have books, movies, theatre, music, graphic and sculptural art, dance. We have devised, and continue to devise, mathematical, geometric, musical, gestural and graphical systems. Most importantly, and fundamentally, we have language, the artifact that has played a major role in the development of virtually every expansion of our ambient world.

It isn't, then, simply a difference in degree that distinguishes us from other creatures: it demands to be thought of rather as a difference in kind. Our experienced world has been transformed by our ability to conceptualize, and thus to create symbolic internal representations of both its elements and its processes.

Those internal representations have two powerful characteristics:

They permit us to transform the raw data from our senses into lasting, retrievable, mentally manipulable information about the world.

They similarly permit us to mull over and ruminate upon that information. That is, they allow us to think about particular aspects of the world when they are not actually present.

What follows?

*We can devise, rehearse, and perform "thought experiments" without any overt action, and without any "real-life" consequences. We can, in fact, play with **ideas**. We can even conceive hypothetical realities, both realistic and fantastic. We can create imaginative fictions for our edification or entertainment, but we can also search for significance and purpose that can transform our endeavors and order our lives.*

The critical difference in kind between humans and other animals is thus:

Other animals have no way of deriving conceptualizations of the world, and thus no way of establishing discrete mentally manipulable representations of its elements, nor abstract notions of its processes.

Philosopher Susanne K. Langer provides us with a wonderful summary:

Human intelligence begins with conception, the prime mental activity: the process of conception always culminates in symbolic expression. A conception is fixed and held only when it has been embodied in a symbol. The genesis of symbolic forms is the odyssey of the mind.[4]

The ability to give symbolic form to our conceptions has had the most extraordinary consequences for humankind. It has not only transformed how we experience everything around us, both animate and inanimate; it has also changed how we experience ourselves.

Most significantly: in becoming able to represent ourselves to ourselves, we have become aware of ourselves *as selves*. We have become *self*-conscious. We have become aware that we, like everything else, animate or inanimate, have an identity that can be investigated, analyzed, and understood in its own right. We *can* look at ourselves as if from the outside. What is more, since we can also represent to ourselves what it is like to be someone else, we have the potential, with imagination, to understand not only how others experience themselves and their worlds, but also how they experience us.

The ability to see ourselves as if from the outside, and to see others (including other creatures and other physical entities), as if from within is arguably—on this planet at least—unique to humankind. The biologist Helmuth Plessner characterized this ability as "off-centeredness," in contrast with what he termed the "centricity" (the exclusive and unselfconscious preoccupation with self) of other animal forms.[5] Unfortunately, the connotations of the word off-centeredness are more evocative of our being off-balance, than of our achieving a better sense of balance in relation to our connectedness with everything else. Unfortunately, too, the available alternative terms have similarly misleading connotations. If we consider off-centeredness to be synonoymous with objectivity, for example, we lose Plessner's attempt to hold on to the wholeness of ourselves. Our language already freights "subjective" and "objective" with connotations of dissociation. What to do? Plessner's translator Marjorie Grene suggested "eccentric" (scarcely an improvement!). The concept is clearly important, however, and it will feature prominently in our future discussion. For our purposes, then, I'm going to suggest we use the phrases connected awareness and off-centeredness as synonyms, trusting that with frequent conscientious use, we can become sufficiently familiar with their implications that we can avoid any knee-jerk tendency to dissociate ourselves both from others and from what we are uncomfortable about in ourselves.

In attending to those implications, however, it is important that we recognize that within ourselves, each sensibility vies with the other. We may as human beings have the power to look at other things and other creatures as if from within; we may have the ability to look at our own selves as if we were another; but this doesn't mean that we all have equal abilities in that regard, nor that we always make use of them. Everything that we try to make sense of as separate human beings can be seen, not only with a connected awareness, but alternatively from the perspective of a unique self-interest. Thus, our questioning of events is frequently not simply "What does this mean?"— a concern derived from the knowledge that any event's significance is affected by its place in the larger context in which it occurs—but rather, "What does this mean for *me?*"—a *very* different question. This latter question may be thought to characterize all animal perception, and so in experiencing it we are as other animals. Even here, however, our humanness adds a further dimension. Unlike other animals, we can be *aware* of asking the question, that is, as a result of our ability to observe our own thinking. Further, our interests themselves can be of a totally symbolic nature. Nevertheless, regardless of whether our concerns arise from the mental processes permitted by symbolic ability or from those unmediated by symbolic representations, if our interests are felt to be at risk, we too will be capable of acting in a purely unselfconscious "centric" manner; in other words, without an observing awareness of ourselves, and without regard to the possible consequences for others, or for anything else.[6]

There seem to be at least three kinds of circumstance in which this is likely to occur:

When, as in early childhood, the concepts that are required for an outside perspective on ourselves are unavailable to us.

When in later years, even though we are capable of connected awareness, we are intensely occupied with getting something done.

When we judge ourselves to be under violent threat.

In the latter two circumstances, off-centered attention may be a distracting liability, since it fosters a delay in action. Delay in the middle of doing something can prevent us from getting it done; delay when we are under serious threat can endanger our very survival. For any adult perceiver, then, it is these last two circumstances that powerfully affect our ability or inability to take account of the full context of our actions, and thus the significance of those actions to others.

There is also a further distinction of the two modes that is critical for us. If we desert the off-centered, connected mode, we set aside—albeit temporarily—our ability to *represent* to ourselves the physical or emotional states of other beings. In such circumstances, then, what those physical or emotional states are will have no significance for our own actions.

Many animals are, of course, affected by the emotional states of others of their species, but as far as we can tell, they experience these states centrically. That is, it seems more accurate to speak of such animals as being flooded with a feeling they experience as their *own*, rather than having a sympathetic outside perspective of it. This is the ability (or, perhaps, we should rather say instinct) for which Langer reserved the much-misused term empathy.[7] Infection by the feeling of others (an unfortunate phrase, but I apologize; at the moment I can't seem to find a better one) certainly exists among human beings also, but our literature on the subject tends to confuse this with an entirely different phenomenon: an *understanding* of the feeling-state of another that is coincident with a profound feeling of sympathetic fellowship. It is this latter ability that our writers on psychotherapy have variously identified as a necessary component for effecting change in others. "Accurate empathy" is the widely used clinical term.[8] Unfortunately the widespread use of the word "empathy" in this second sense obliterates the crucial distinction between our being capable of a contextually aware off-centered appraisal on the one hand, and subjective, centric immersion on the other. To retain an awareness of this crucial difference, I shall use the word "sympathy" to designate the ability to recognize and re-constitute in ourselves the feeling-state of another, and the word "empathy" for the mergence of our identity with that of another; in other words, experiencing the feeling-state of the other as if it were our own.

Certainly, we can only have true sympathy if we can identify the feeling-state of the other, in order either to recall in ourselves what that feeling is like, or, on the basis of our familiarity with similar states, to *imagine* what it is like. This capability *requires* that we temporarily forgo preoccupation with ourselves. In short, identifying and being sympathetic to a feeling experienced by another is different from being suffused with the feeling that we have identified. We may be powerfully affected, but in ways having more to do with our own prior experience of a particular emotion than with a true understanding of the specific, subjectively experienced emotion in the person—or, indeed, animal —with whom we are being sympathetic. Erroneously believing that we understand how another person feels probably occurs much more frequently than we would wish. Even correctly identifying a person's feeling doesn't inevitably mean that we know how it feels. The external signs of grief, for example, are virtually unmistakable, but if we have not experienced deep personal grief, our depth of understanding is limited.

Langer's definition of empathy is that it is "an involuntary breach of individual separateness." By contrast, if we experience powerful feelings as the result of a dramatic performance in the theatre, or in a movie, or even upon reading a very affecting story (as I did myself just a couple of days ago), we can draw back and observe our identification with the characters involved; indeed, we may well use our experience of such feelings as evidence of the quality of the fiction. We are thus still aware of our observer status, our non-involvement in the action. We may call this, perhaps, an objective understanding of our subjective state. If, however, in response to nonfictional life circumstances (or possibly in response to a powerful fiction) we become powerfully affected or even overwhelmed by feelings that originate in others, and take them on as our own (are, in a word, "infected" by them), then two other sorts of summary are possible.

If we are frequently or pervasively permeated with the feeling-states of others, it is possible to think of ourselves as *undifferentiated* from those others. In particular, Otto Pollak refers to the phenomenon—when found in the members of disturbed families—as an "undifferentiated ego-mass"; that is, a *merged* identity.[9] In other words, psychotherapists will often diagnose the condition as a failure to achieve an independent coherent sense of self.[10] In such cases, merged identity is not so much evidence of a breach of individual separateness, but rather of a failure to reach it.

Is this inability to differentiate self from other only characteristic of relationships within deeply immature families? As a pervasive identification, it seems likely that it is. However, there are in human society many occasions that permit and even encourage the merging of one's individual identity with that of a larger group. Similarly, it is one of the characteristics of our own time that people whom we can suspect of being unfulfilled in their own lives attempt to take on the persona of some public figure who represents to them an idealized fulfillment of their own thwarted ambitions or fantasies. We should be clear that such phenomena have a very different dynamic than that involved in our sympathetic appreciation of a person who seems to embody the ideals that we ourselves aspire to realize. In those of us with a flawed sense of self, it seems likely that there is nevertheless at root a deep common urge, perhaps generated by an instinctive dread of isolation. It might, indeed, be considered further evidence of the situation so poignantly defined by John Donne:

> No man is an island, entire of itself; every man is a piece of the continent, a part of the main: if a clod be washed away by the sea, Europe is the less, as well as if a promontory were, as well as if a manor of thy friends or thine own were; any man's death diminishes me, because I am involved in mankind; and therefore never send to know for whom the bell tolls; it tolls for thee.[11]

In Donne's sense, then, it is scarcely unhealthy to be powerfully affected by the pain or the joy of other human beings.

Indeed, we all know of people whose achievements are of the sort that result from dedicating their lives to others. That they can do so, however, is more likely to be an indicator of powerful connected awareness of both feeling and context than of an absence of differentiation. To be totally merged with the identity of another would exclude any possibility of seeing that person's situation from another perspective, or, indeed, of seeing oneself as a differentiated self.

A merged undifferentiated identity would seem to exclude not only the possibility of independent fulfillment, but also any true participation in realizing the communal fulfillment of humankind.[12]

If a secure, differentiated identity is an essential factor in healthy, communal interaction, what can we say is a healthy balance of sympathy and separation, of communion and independence? This is perhaps the central social question for humanity. The manner of our relating to one another is uniquely and indelibly marked: on the one hand by the symbolizing abilities that permit us the possibility of understanding ourselves and others, and on the other by an instinctual, non-self-observing self-interest that is ignorant of who that self really is, and therefore of who others really are as well.

For humankind, in short, symbolic ability enables us to engage and cooperate with each other in a manner that is simply unavailable to other creatures. The sharing of our conceptualizations with one another has brought about the miracle of language, with its opportunities for generating common understandings, exploring complex ideas, and fostering cooperative endeavor. The communication of feelings and ideas has enriched all of us, far beyond the potential of any individual alone. It is in sharing with one another our perceptions, perspectives, opinions, images, models, techniques, visions, and values that we constitute the individual and collective cultures of humanity.

In making sense of ourselves, then, we have to take account of our collective reality. Any one of us may be restricted as to our symbolic capabilities, but our membership in the human collective means that we can not only benefit from the extensions of the human ambient permitted by the discoveries of others, but also have a part in contributing to them. Few of the contrivances that now seem inescapably necessary for our living enjoyable lives could have been brought into existence without protracted cooperative effort between groups of people bending their motives to a common purpose.

There is also, however, a virtually inevitable downside to human symbolic ability: we are able to form *misrepresentations* of ourselves, the world, and one another. The resulting vicissitudes of human cooperation and conflict will demand our attention soon enough, however. For the moment, let us take stock rather of the enormously empowering potential of symbolic mental processes.

We can summarize, I think, as follows:

1. We may extend Von Uexküll's conceptual scheme in the human case by proposing that for each human being, and for human beings collectively, there exists a "conceptual ambient."[13] The conceptual ambient consists of the currently existing concepts available for mental representations of reality, including abstract ideas about its nature and its functioning. Clearly, the conceptual ambient of humanity as a whole is larger than that of any individual.

   Similarly, in any particular circumstance—for an individual as for any particular grouping of individuals—there is a *functional* conceptual ambient consisting of the concepts available at that time and in that situation, but also a *potential* conceptual ambient (one that might result from further education, experience, or simply more concentrated thinking beyond the bounds of existing conceptualizations).

2. The conceptual ambient of each of us has similarities to, and differences from, the conceptual ambients of others.

3. We can communicate about these similarities and differences, and thus have the power to affect the conceptual ambients of others, either by extending them or modifying them. Each of us thus has potential access to the conceptual ambients of others, and therefore has the possibility of increasing his or her own conceptual range by indirect experience. This allows for human beings to educate one another without being constrained, as other animals are, by circumstantial limits to opportunities for immediate (i.e., *un-mediated*) direct-experience learning.

4. The ability to communicate to one another both our discoveries and our perspectives means that the range and subtlety of the human conceptual ambient are progressively modified over time. Advances of human potential are thus transmissible not only within generations, but also from one generation to the next. The genetic evolution of our kind is thus supplemented by a conceptual evolution. Each human being's inheritance is, in consequence, not simply phylogenetic, but cultural.

5. Since we have the ability to modify one another's conceptual ambients, different human beings can concentrate on developing different highly specialized areas of conceptual exploration because we can assume that similar exploration is occurring elsewhere also, and that our own work will find a place in the cumulative development of human knowledge. As far as we know, other animals cannot communicate to others of their kind what each of them has individually learned, except by personal example. Although there is also currently an alternative hypothesis, it remains controversial, and, as far as I have been able to discover, no convincing confirmatory evidence for it has been found.[14] Let us accept,

then, that an individual animal can learn from its own kind only by direct experience and observation. There is no such restriction on human beings.

6. The conceptual ambient of humankind is, hypothetically, infinitely extendable. Can anyone be found who seriously believes there will come a moment when humankind will understand everything there is to be known?

7. In any circumstance where there is a natural limit to an individual's perceptual and action ambients, symbolic processes may permit us to transcend those limits.

8. The potential range of a person's conceptual ambient is restricted by that person's available intelligence, just as its actual range tends to be restricted by the arenas in which one has chosen to exercise that intelligence.[15] In modern societies the demands of specialization are often sufficiently great that innovative thinkers in a particular field may well reveal surprising shortcomings in their ability to understand what is going on elsewhere.

9. An event, circumstance, process, or phenomenon for which a human being does not have concepts can be considered *not* to exist as a factor in that person's conscious understanding of the world. A human being's ambient is thus defined as much by that person's inventory of available concepts as an animal's ambient is defined by its instincts and its preconceptual abilities. It is the range, richness, precision, and versatility of a particular person's conceptual ambient that determine the depth, subtlety, and validity of the kind of sense that person can make.

Figure One illustrates the role of each ambient in contributing to one's mental representation of the world.[16]

FIGURE ONE

THE CONSTITUENTS OF AN INDIVIDUAL'S WORLD

Perceptual Ambient
(The world that can be registered by one's senses)

↓

The total
mental representation
of oneself and the world
brought about
by the interaction of
all three ambients

Conceptual Ambient   *Action Ambient*
(The world of available   (The world of action
mental representations)   permitted by one's anatomy)

In evaluating the overall effect on humanity of its possession of a conceptual ambient, it is difficult to overstate the importance of the difference between human and animal representations. However, it is easy on that account to undervalue the similarities. Given that in some circumstances our symbolic abilities either desert us, or fail to meet the circumstances of the case, we would do well to understand better the manner in which our pre-symbolic sensibilities function. After all, the extraordinary complexity and diversity of animal behavior should be ample evidence that the pre-symbolic mode of being in the world has a powerful logic of its own. Once again, Langer has an apt summary:

> The reason why animals, operating without concepts or symbols, can function as effectively as men might do in similar situations, and sometimes more effectively than men could, is that their major instinctive acts are . . . unconfused by any awareness of merely possible exigencies, possible errors, or thoughts of other possible acts.[17]

In other words, and to quote Russell Hoban's evocative phrase, animals other than humans do not carry "sharks in the mind."[18] We do carry sharks in the mind, but we also carry a lot more there than can easily be summarized metaphorically. We may at times be confused by the multiplicity of choices available to us, but at others we are energized by the opportunities for fulfillment they offer. It's clearly important, then, to examine more fully the nature of our symbolizations. They are a good deal more complex than you might think.

3

Belief

WHAT IS CONTAINED in any human mind is a complex mixture. The character of that mixture derives from the interaction of several distinct elements. Those elements are:

The instincts we possess in common by virtue of our membership in the human species,

The abilities and tendencies we all of us possess by virtue of our unique individual genetic endowment, and

The modes of understanding permitted by our preconceptual mental representations, our symbolic mental representations, and our physical and emotional experience.

The relative weight of these factors will clearly vary enormously in each of us, but since any analysis of the mixture or its constituent elements requires that we use propositional thought, it seems important to further our enterprise by assessing the extent to which propositional thought, and, indeed, language itself, jointly determine the shape of what we have come to believe.

Language is not the only influence on such shape, however. Since it is attractive to believe that any kind of understanding can be summarized in language, we must be very careful to avoid seducing ourselves into believing that language itself *determines* all such understandings. It is true that each person's experienced world depends on the nature of the concepts that person has come to use to understand it. But it is equally true that a person's individual experience of the meaning of such conceptualizations is profoundly influenced by the nature of his or her prior pre-conceptual learning. For every individual one of us, early learning occurs *without conceptual form*, and so, although a skilled observer or interlocutor could summarize such learning in propositional form (that is, in the form of an assertion about the nature of the other person's beliefs) it is unlikely that the original learner would. Early direct-experience learning occurs when one is in *centric* mode (that is, without being in an observing position in relation to oneself). When each of us is later able to develop the awareness of self and other that distinguishes us from other animals, one's familiarity with oneself will tend to curtail any curiosity about the nature of personal beliefs derived from pre-conceptual direct experiences—unless, of course, later experience provides some compelling reason to do otherwise. Few of us will question how it has come about that we are quick or slow to anger, optimistic or pessimistic about outcomes, trustful or distrustful of instruction, willing or unwilling to take up physical or intellectual challenges, diligent or dilatory in meeting expectations.

Pre-conceptual direct experiences affect not only what we believe about ourselves, but also what we believe about others. "People have always eaten people!" protest the outraged cannibals in the song by Michael Flanders and Donald Swann.[1] (It is, by the way, a humbling exercise to imagine oneself protesting similarly about the obviousness of beliefs that we ourselves hold!)

The very first beliefs of all of us result from whether we register the world as a responsive, supportive, friendly, benevolent place, or a hostile one. Extra-uterine life suddenly requires of us an utterly different engagement with it than intra-uterine life did. Does this new world respond favorably to our initial groping engagement with it? Unfavorably? Or does it simply not seem to respond to us at all? Our own respondent feelings, which we may perhaps call "emotional cognitions," are primarily registered through our experience of our significance to those who are closest to us. Do they cuddle us when we are cold? Do they suckle us when we are hungry? Do they hold us with tender joy and comforting sounds? Or not? What sense do *we* make of the sense *they* make of us? These cognitions remain probably the most powerful internal representations for all of us, and they are also likely to remain unavailable to our later conscious awareness unless they precipitate for us tremendous personal cost. With sufficient persistence in experience, those cognitions take up residence in us as unquestioned (because originally unquestionable) conviction.

Although we must clearly be cautious, then, not to underestimate the importance of extra-linguistic factors in contributing to our mental representations of the world, we must nevertheless give sufficient weight to the fact that language apparently provides us with the most powerful, coherent, inclusive, and systematic means of investigating how those representations are formed. It is also true that different languages produce different kinds of potentials for understanding. However, for the moment, let us stay with the very broadest generalization. All languages share similarities. What, then, are the kinds of frameworks that all verbal languages both enable us and constrain us to think in?

Clearly, propositional language itself is inconceivable without our already having been able to identify and symbolize discrete entities or categories of experience. It appears that such categorization can both precede and be coincident with the recognition of relationships and of causality, but, whatever the case, identifying discrete categories of experience clearly simplifies enormously our mental handling of what would otherwise be overwhelmingly large amounts of data from our senses, and thus increases the acuity of what we can perceive and the richness of its detail. Any categorization, regardless of what criteria of selection initially determined its form, necessarily contributes to our being able to discern how discrete things and groups of things relate to each other. More abstractly, that discernment leads to *propositions* about those relationships and the processes that characterize them. Such propositions lead to the development of *systems* of understanding, or in other words, to networks of inter-related *assertions* about the nature of reality. It was perfectly understandable that those cannibals in the Flanders and Swann song should attribute the anti-cannibalism feelings of the young protestor to some person that he'd already eaten.

Properly, even the discernment of any discrete thing—be it a feeling, a physical entity, a process, an event, an attribute, or an abstract idea (a principle of some kind, for example)—may itself be represented symbolically as a proposition. The initial form of this would be something like "This bundle of impressions indicates a 'this,'" or, perhaps more prior, "This bundle of impressions *feels* different from other bundles." (That is, in the first instance, treating the possibility of a valid concept as itself a *hypothesis*.) Animals clearly function perfectly well within particular limits without having concepts. They can identify many physical signs in their environments that have particular meaning for them. Some may even offer "gifts" that have a particular significance to potential sexual partners. To *assert* anything about any percept, however, would require that it be retrievable mentally; that is, that it be *conceptualized,* and thus become present in the mind as an idea *without* the necessity of the perceived object being present. Langer's account strongly suggests that we couldn't think *about* anything at all, let alone formulate propositions about it, unless we had already made it available for mental use by symbolizing it in some way. As far as we know, this is specifically what other animals cannot do.

Again, however, we must be careful. Systematic thinking requires conceptualization of some kind, but the thinking that precedes conceptualization is extremely difficult to characterize. We know a great deal about the way children move from rudimentary conceptualizations to the more subtle and versatile distinctions characteristic of adult thinking,[2] but we struggle to understand how any of us manage to transcend the limitations of our prior conceptualizations and the verbal propositions permitted by them. Alfred North Whitehead, for example, remarked that "sometimes a thought won't enter words."[3] Similarly, Albert Einstein described his own thought processes as being akin to the sensation of muscle movements.[4] Both Einstein and Whitehead were fully aware that they were nevertheless *thinking*.

For the simpler circumscribed purposes of our current task, however, let us restrict ourselves to describing the structural nature of propositional thought itself. Assertions about the existence of entities, their attributes, and the nature of the relationships between them, constitute a particular form of internal representation. They summarize what we hold in our minds as beliefs about the world.[5] The very first assertions of any individual, as those of the earliest individuals of our kind, would clearly be simple, and necessarily keyed to the sense experiences from which they were derived; but later, both the concepts themselves, and the propositions about the relationships between them, can and have become very complex. In order to clarify the situation somewhat, then, and notwithstanding the complexities involved in the development of logical thought, let us suggest a simple practical way to categorize our propositions.

Propositions (beyond those that paraphrase, specify, or define the concepts themselves) seem to be of three basic types. Each refers to a different order of reality. Thus:

1. There are propositions about the "is-ness" of the world: that is, the world as it seems to present itself to us as an actual phenomenon. Propositions in this area can be concerned not only with the world of purely physical things, but also with the world of human relationships, enterprises, and ideas: "Blood is thicker than water." Both kinds codify what we believe to be true about the world as it appears to us, that is, as a stable entity, an apparent "given." I shall call both kinds propositions about *fact,* and their area of reference *factual belief.*

2. There are propositions about *process*, or *processes*: that is, about how things work, how they come about, how they function, how they affect one another. In this area, too, propositions may refer not only to the purely physical world, but also to the world of human activities, which is imbued with symbolic meaning: "A stitch in time saves nine." Thus, how people and their symbolic systems *function* is a sub-category of such propositions, with the designation of *motives* a major element. Propositions about process can also be thought of as having to do with the area of action and result, or with cause and effect. I shall call this area of reference that of *process belief*. Since beliefs about how things come about are also beliefs about how to make them come about, beliefs in this area have strongly *prescriptive* implications, in that they "tell" us how to act in order to produce a particular kind of result. Few of us, in any culture, would turn up for a job interview without giving due care to our personal grooming. No athlete would expect success in competition without careful and extended prior training. Only a highly trained sailor or perhaps an utterly desperate refugee would risk putting to sea in a violent storm. It is worthy of at least brief remark, too, that, since a major concern of us all is that we be effective in our lives, prescriptive advice is the preferred persuasive tool of advertisers, who can be particularly adept at promulgating prescriptive beliefs that serve their own profit—"If you want to get ahead, get a hat!"

3. There are propositions about *value*: these are concerned with preferred states of reality, or preferred modes and outcomes of action. They designate the area of a person's interests and commitment. I shall call the area of relevance for these propositions that of *value belief*. It is the area of human concern that is most heavily imbued with *feeling*. In the human arena, indeed, values constitute the matrix within which are set the motivational imperatives that derive from our moral

convictions. Although it may bear repeating that decisions about how to act will always be affected in any circumstance by one's assessment of threat or of opportunity, powerful moral elements may carry more weight than purely pragmatic considerations. In Shakespeare's *Hamlet*, Polonius' advice to Laertes is prototypical:

> This above all, to thine own self be true,
> And it must follow, as the night the day,
> Thou canst not then be false to any man.

I am very aware that, in my own search for a simple statement of the general principles underlying any propositional structure, my designations necessarily bear the stamp of my own subject–predicate language. It's important to recognize, then, that the semantic and syntactic characteristics of languages other than our own might well suggest more subtle differentiations and significantly different emphasis.

It is, in fact, hard to overstate the profound effect the familiarity with one's own language has, both on the kind of sense one can make, and also upon one's ability to understand the modes of thought, let alone the beliefs, of someone from another culture, even with the benefit of apparently adequate translation. In short, it is important for us to be mindful that different languages may represent particular aspects of experience and thought differently, and that some of these differences may be critical for a deeper understanding, both of the external world and of ourselves.[6]

The power of languages to influence radically the very nature of one's apparent beliefs has been convincingly shown in experiments with bilingual subjects, who, in widely used standard psychological tests (devised, nevertheless, we should remind ourselves, within the constraints of particular cultural assumptions) seemed to reveal different personalities, depending on which language was used.[7] I myself find that I feel like a totally different person when I think and speak in French. What would the thoughts in this book have been like, I wonder, if my native language had not been English, but Urdu, or Arabic, or Inuktitut?

Notwithstanding these reservations, however, it should be apparent that it is the propositions we live by—in both their content and their form, and regardless of our awareness or unawareness of them—that constitute who we experience ourselves to be. That is, they summarize not only what we believe about the world, but also what we believe about ourselves in relation to it. I shall take this continuity of belief to be synonymous with one's sense of personal identity.

However, this sense of one's identity, the sense of who one truly is, is not necessarily conscious. We may indeed be self-deceptive in the characteristics we attribute to ourselves, whether fondly or otherwise. Knowing ourselves is probably an aspiration for most of us, but its fullest realization is another matter. It is not an easy commitment to make. However:

*Any proposition that, even subliminally, we experience as antago-nistic to our cumulative belief, to our own particular continuity of meaning, can be experienced as a potential threat to our identity; that is, to whom we **feel** ourselves to be.*

This is true even if our accumulated continuity of meaning is a negative one (that is, one that summarizes our identity as unsuccessful). We can think of a negative continuity of meaning as a response to life experiences that have curtailed our sense of effectiveness to a tightly circumscribed mode and area of action. Such a negative identity would seem to require a severe restriction of what we can perhaps think of as "life-space." Lynch, for example, asserted that "uprooted persons, those who suffer shock, or those whose realistic futures are terrifying or completely unpredictable, will withdraw into a narrow present." By contrast, "It is when local time, local place and ourselves are secure that we are ready to face challenge, complexity, vast space, and the enormous future."[8] There could scarcely be a clearer summary of the manner in which one's security of identity affects the size, as well as the character, of one's world.

In short: the more secure one's sense of self, the larger the world with which we are able to deal, and the greater our ability to consider it otherwise than as simply the context of our subjective purpose or the sole determiner of the quality of our existence.

The security of one's sense of self, then, significantly determines what circumstances or events are reacted to as threats to one's identity, or opportunities for its fuller realization. It is not only the obvious oppressions of one's environment, however, that may result in the restriction of one's life-space. Imagined or anticipated restrictions may have power in no way inferior to that of the terrifying realistic futures spoken of by Lynch. In other words, restrictions of life-space may be attributable to the way we actually *think* about things, rather than to our actual circumstances.

The most important aspect of a person's identity is revealed in his or her stance in relation to life: that is, the person's *attitude,* which—notwithstanding any genetic factors or actual brain injury—encapsulates what that person has cumulatively come to believe. This attitude contains one's "terms of engagement" with the world: one's optimism or pessimism about outcomes, one's fear or eagerness to engage, one's preference for modes of engagement, one's persistence and determination (or lack of them), one's preference in relationships as well as one's behavior in them, one's preference in activities, one's threshold of joy and of surfeit, one's moral stance in relation to others, one's sense of responsibilities and rights (in fact, everything that has to do with the way we participate in life, because of the sense we have made of it).

For reasons that will become apparent, I shall term the sum of one's beliefs about the world (that is, those propositions about category, about fact, about process, about value, that are held to be true) one's framing of reality, or more briefly, one's "frame."[9] It is by my framing of reality (that is, my superimposition on reality of my beliefs about its structure and character) that I enable myself to choose what to pay attention to, decide how to act, and feel good or bad about myself and the world. In so doing, I control my world and feel effective in relation to it, if only to a necessarily limited degree.

I experience my understanding itself, in fact, as a form of effective action.

Although theoretically the propositions containing my beliefs are modifiable through new experiences that corroborate, refine, or refute them, beliefs that have apparently worked well enough in the past will have accumulated sufficient weight to be not easily shifted. Indeed, once I've used a particular formulation, and found it to be useful beyond a certain critical threshold of adequacy, it immediately possesses greater apparent validity than untried formulations, and if the life-circumstances upon which it bears are urgent and unremitting, I'm unlikely to spend time searching for a more effective formulation. My acting upon the formulation takes greater priority. This constitutes, indeed, an essential given of our human situation: the ever-varying tension between the need to make "correct" formulations and the need to make them soon enough to be of immediate use.

Our ability to discern whether our formulations are correct or not depends in part on the persuasiveness of the corroboration or lack of corroboration we receive about them, but also, naturally, on our awareness of the costs of error. Feedback that irrefutably tells us that our very survival depends on changing a formulation that we had previously taken to be correct would clearly get us to change our view in short order. Feedback that is more ambiguous would undoubtedly be less powerful. As Kenneth Burke puts it,

If people believe a belief, and live, the fact of their survival tends
to prove the adequacy of the belief. This is so because wrong beliefs
are not necessarily fatal, and because even dangerous beliefs may
be of such a sort that they cannot be proved dangerous.[10]

We are not yet ready for a full listing of the ways in which error
can occur, but we can, even at this point, recognize a difference
in the nature of feedback coming from the physically experienced
world (that is, the world as directly experienced via the senses),
and the world as experienced via the mediation of symbolized
representations (that is, the world as indirectly experienced).

Like most animals—except, obviously, those driven by instinct
alone—our first learning about the physical world derives from
our immediate sense experience of it, and our awareness of its
response or lack of response to our own actions. This is *practical*
learning; it occurs relatively quickly, partly because the physical
laws that govern our existence are inexorable, and partly because
the feedback from direct experience of the physical world is usually quick, immediate, and powerful. We quickly learn what is
pleasurable and what is not; few of us reach out eagerly to touch
a naked flame more than once.

The situation is similar for emotional learning. To be born
into a hostile or emotionally sterile world may, in fact, fundamentally stunt one's potential engagement with life, and in
extreme cases stifle it entirely. The feedback experienced by some
unfortunate infants shouts to them, "You are not wanted here!"
Unless this circumstance is quickly changed, they die.[11]

While most of us are unlikely to have experienced such completely devastating early circumstances, many have undoubtedly
endured situations that they have survived only at the cost of
marked debilities or aberrations of spirit. The ramifications of
such outcomes are, of course, of enormous importance for all of
us. Whether we can come fully to grips with those ramifications
crucially depends on our awareness or unawareness of their costs,
and on how much we *care* about them. The visibility or invisibility

of those costs and whether we are willing to tolerate them is thus critically important to our deciding whether or not we are willing to give adequate attention to the circumstances and processes that produced them. In recent times, the collective identity of citizens of the United States was profoundly threatened by a growing collective awareness that its government was actively promoting torture of those held to be involved in terrorist activity.

The situation regarding feedback in the area of indirect experience (that is, experience *mediated* by conceptual thought) is more complex. Briefly put, it is simply easier to be wrong about the meaning of such feedback. This is not only because the processes of conceptualization and propositional thought can result in erroneous ideas about reality, but also because feedback in the area of symbolic representations can be deliberately formulated to deceive. In short, we can lie. We can lie to others; others can lie to us. To make it even more fraught, we can lie to ourselves. Both error and deception will require our greater attention shortly.

For the moment, let's consider more carefully the nature of our beliefs, and in particular the degree of our commitment to them. How can we come to understand better the kind of circumstances in which openness or closure is favored? What determines whether a belief is easily relinquished, or stubbornly maintained?

4

Survival, and Opportunity

THE ASCENDANT MOTIVES of any individual life form are to survive and produce offspring. Both are necessary for the continuing survival and development of its kind.

This is as true for us human beings as it is for any creature, but with the added complexity that each person's instinct for survival may apply equally as strongly to the *protection of identity.* In other words, *in the symbolic arena we may be just as concerned with protecting what we believe, as in the physical arena we are with protecting our simple existence.* A perceived threat to the continuity of what we believe will—although in differing degrees, and depending on our assessment of the nature of the threat—trigger a protective response. The quality of our commitment to the beliefs we live by can thus be characterized as having different "levels," different thresholds of vulnerability to feedback. Thus:

In the deepest layers of our framings of the world, we have all accumulated sets of assumptions about life that are relatively stable, and that we usually neither expose nor question. These assumptions may apply to any type of proposition, including conceptualizations themselves, as well as to the propositions about fact, process, and value permitted by them. Some of these assumptions will be based on one's accumulated direct sensual experience of physical reality; some, however, will be based rather on indirect (symbolically mediated) experience. There is always, of course, a direct component in mediated experience—as, for example, in hearing the sound of a word, and the expression given to it by a speaker, or seeing it written on a page—but these characteristics of a mediating symbol are virtually insignificant (except in poetry, or other artistic endeavors, where the form itself contributes to the meaning it can carry, or in situations where there is an incongruity between the form of a sentence and the manner in which it is spoken). In language, it is the literal meaning of sentences that has significance for us, rather than how they sound or how they appear. It's again a bit more complicated than that—indeed, quite a bit more complicated—but we'll save the complications for later.

Direct experience rather obviously eventuates in practical learning about our physical environment. It is also, however, the source of our deepest emotional learning: our sense of growing in a friendly and supportive world, for example, rather than in a hostile or disaffirming one. Whether we feel affirmed or disaffirmed in our first experiences of the world, then, depends in large part not only on the actual physical circumstances into which each of us was born, but also on the sense of those circumstances that our elders and progenitors were themselves able to make. That sense would also be a powerful determinant of our progenitors' attitudes towards us; and it is those attitudes that in turn strongly affect our own fundamental learning about our place in human society. Moreover, in the very early stages of our experiencing of the world, it is unlikely that our infant sensibilities would permit more subtle distinctions of the meaning of attitudes towards us than a crude "feels good" or "feels bad."

Clearly, although the circumstances of this first direct-experience learning may remain a dominant factor in all our later sense-making, subsequent modifications will also bear the stamp of indirect experience. As we acquire language, we acquire with it not only the ability to reach beyond the boundary of direct experience, but also—at first unknowingly—the formal assumptions of the representational system of language itself. This applies also to our learning the assumptions underlying non-linguistic representational systems.[1] We are thus not only exposed to the cumulative sense-making of our elders, but also, unknowingly, to the formal and structural assumptions of the symbolic systems we have inherited from them. These latter assumptions will consist of the formal conventions characteristic of the particular symbol-system in use, or rules (like syntax in language), which determine the range and versatility of the system, and which consequently foster preferential modes of thought. We may call these latter symbol-assumptions *instrumental*, since symbols are the instruments we use to transform our raw experience of the world into conscious sense.

It will be apparent that instrumental symbol-assumptions tend, for most of us, most of the time, to be transparent to our awareness. That is, we are unaware that the ways in which we think about things, devise representations of them and form statements about them, contain assumptions about the adequacy of the concepts or images being used (we may call these "semantic" assumptions), and assumptions about the way such concepts or images can be manipulated intellectually in a formal system of thought. (We may call these "syntactic" assumptions.)

In a way, our concepts and the rules for employing them may be considered to be like lenses that permit us to focus on a content that lies beyond them. Obviously, such concepts and rules *must* be transparent, as we would be unable to think constructively about anything at all if we had to re-evaluate our conceptual assumptions at every instant. However, since faulty assumptions—whether semantic or syntactic—can vitiate our thinking, it is important that we be able to gain access to them for purposes of revision. When we are able to do this, the symbols, as well as the systematic structures in which they function, become *opaque* (in other words, perceivable, and thus available to examination). Clearly, when our symbols and our combinatorial logic are opaque, we cannot look through them to what they designate, but are stopped at an intermediate point. When focusing our attention upon the interior of a lens, we cannot look through it. Accordingly, it has to be a pretty severe circumstance to cause us momentarily to concentrate on our instruments. This is particularly true, and ironically so, for my own profession (and hence, in part, one of the reasons for this book), but it is also true for any activity, the interruption of which could be thought to cause great hardship. The greater hardships stemming from inadequate conceptual formulations do not, unfortunately, leap into view as easily.

It is probably only too obvious that whether we felt affirmed or disaffirmed in our first encounters with the world powerfully affects the degree to which we might subsequently be willing to question our fundamental assumptions. On the one hand, it is obvious that most of us attach our sense of identity in sometimes very complex ways to our lineage, our ancestors, our nationalities, our gender, and our ethnicity. Our continuity of meaning thus potentially includes as a positive factor our physical, emotional, and cognitive inheritance. That is, we can feel that our continuity transcends our own time: that it is part of a continuum of which the past, the present, and the future are the essential phases. On the other hand, an identity can be established on the basis of a rejection of those aspects of our inheritance that our experience has led us to feel are alien to our own sensibility. Here too, however, continuity of meaning is potentially critical, but here it is more likely to take the shape of a continuity of affiliation with others, both past and present, who are struggling, or who have struggled in much the same manner as we ourselves to free themselves from the constraints of their inheritance. In both cases, it is nevertheless the emotional and symbolic value of one's own identity that is felt to be at stake. Our affiliations, whether across time or in space, will simply illustrate, or provide the context for our own struggles to affirm who we sense ourselves to be. Who we sense ourselves to be is also, of course, a component factor in the identity of humankind itself.

Following the sociologist Erving Goffman, I shall call the assumptions that make up our most fundamental beliefs "primary frame assumptions."[2] Their nature has been dramatically summarized by Ludwig Wittgenstein:

> The general form of propositions is "This is how things are." That is the kind of proposition that one repeats to oneself countless times. One thinks that one is tracing the outline of the thing's nature over and over again, and one is merely tracing around the frame through which we look at it.[3]

We should add that the connotative resources of the word "frame" itself further suggest the very structure of a belief, and not simply the linguistic container for it.

Since we confidently hold our primary frame assumptions to be true, we rarely question them in the course of everyday living. Any experience that is incongruent with them may therefore be considered (and not necessarily consciously, as we shall see) a threat to identity, and therefore resisted. All of us can, and frequently do, use a variety of defensive maneuverings to keep these fundamental beliefs intact. Such maneuverings may occur solely in our thought processes, but they may also appear in how we choose to act, both symbolically and physically. If, following such procedures, the discrepancies or incongruities refuse to be dismissed—or perhaps increase, thus constituting data that are massively contrary to our primary frame assumptions—then either we shift the balance of our beliefs to absorb the new evidence, *or* our defensive maneuvers themselves become proportionately massive. Often, indeed, it is the very massiveness of such defenses that provides an interlocutor or observer with evidence that a profound basic identity-assumption is under threat.

It is understandable that we should strongly resist changing the assumptions that we experience as being crucial to our sense of identity. Indeed, even in science—where there exist rigorous standards for the weighing of evidence—it is well-documented that, again and again, thinkers and researchers who have themselves been instrumental in expanding the boundaries of human knowledge have found it impossible to entertain hypotheses that threatened their own primary frame beliefs. Einstein's much-quoted dictum about the impossibility of a dice-playing God is perhaps the most well-known example, but there are many others, widely chronicled.[4] Indeed, Wittgenstein himself (attached as he was to the rigorous investigation of linguistic forms), famously prescribed only silence for that of which we cannot speak.[5] Did the possibilities for understanding inherent in painting, sculpture, music, dance, and other artistic and expressive forms lurk beyond the linguistic horizon he had at first unknowingly and probably ambivalently imposed on himself?

As the cumulative understanding available to humankind advances through the ages, it is tempting in any given age to discern in any transitory manifestation of resistance to particular ideas a new and epoch-specific pattern of closed-mindedness. There is obviously an element of truth in this, but it is perhaps more useful to suggest, I think, that each age illustrates anew the prevailing pattern of human struggle to discover more satisfactory schemes of understanding. In any age, this struggle is characterized by the resistance of older, historically prestigious beliefs to retain their sway against new discoveries resulting both from scientific enquiry and changes in the framing of the basic questions of philosophy. The ascendancy of purely religious modes of explanation may no longer be as prevalent in our own age as in the past, but "science" and "religion" are still at loggerheads as paradigms of explanation. Our attachments may thus not only be to spurious explanatory schemes that have served a useful practical purpose, but also to those serving particular psychological needs. It seems likely that none of us is ever totally free of such attachments.

"*Above*" the layer of our primary frame assumptions, we also have a level of classification in which we allow ourselves to take a more enquiring attitude towards discrepant experience. That is, we are willing to ask questions and entertain hypotheses about the meaning of experiences for which we have not yet accumulated primary frame assumptions. Similarly, we may have tentatively held beliefs in which we remain somewhat uncertain, and which we are therefore willing to expose to the hardships of contrary evidence. It is apparent, too, that we will be more open-minded about matters that are of no immediate or significant importance to us. Indeed, we may be completely indifferent to the significance of disconfirming evidence for hypotheses that do not seem to touch on our interests. Few of us, I suspect, would do more than simply shrug our shoulders if some specialist revealed to us evidence that our orbit about the sun was some million miles or so greater than we had previously thought.

Yet further above the layers of primary frame assumptions and hypothesis testing there is a layer that can be almost without boundary in the creative person (and thus, I dare say, potentially in all of us). It is a layer where the person is alert for new experiences and hypotheses about the world, and perhaps even seeking them. It is a layer in which one's attention may range from floating free to becoming highly focused, as the circumstances seem to require. In short, it matters little whether the searching be initiated adventitiously or willfully, for each complements the other, and the common factor in both is *curiosity*. It is curiosity that pushes at the boundaries of human experience, and pries at the cracks in our understanding, and it is curiosity that signifies a secure, off-centered engagement with life.

This third kind of openness has been described as "speculative," even "anarchic,"[6] and so it is almost always potentially threatening to someone's established order of belief. (Someone else's, of course!) Whatever the case, such openness is virtually never pre-occupied with safety. Nor is it likely to be associated with anything other than an active engagement with the world. Passivity is alien to it. Receptivity is not. Its absence from human society is a telling indicator of decadence and stagnation. It was in this regard that Whitehead pithily remarked that the notable creative quality of the ancient Greek thinkers was "the genius to be astonished."[7]

In taking stock of this secure open-mindedness, however, it is important that we be able to distinguish it from a mode of being-in-the-world that superficially resembles it, but is in reality a manifestation of a particular kind of closed-mindedness. This mode is distinguishable by its obsessive rejection of any type of generally accepted belief. It equates the rejection of established modes as itself creative, regardless of the contrary evidence. It tends to foster political, personal, and instrumental allegiances that unite disaffected members of society. Contrary to the open-minded seeking of truth, however, it rarely has any program beyond the destruction of established belief, or established conventions of social order. It tears down; it does not build up. It gives a transitory feeling of effectiveness to destructive activity. It associates personal integrity with reaction and disaffiliation. As with other mistaken modes of being-in-the-world, however, its specific attractiveness needs to be understood, for it clearly provides a powerfully convincing motive for those whose practices are based upon it.[8]

There is, too, another variation of the critical mode. It consists of standing conspicuously at the edge of other people's convictions, and inserting one's scalpel at all the points of incongruity in the other person's thought. It seems to represent a withdrawal from willingness to take responsibility for asserting on one's own behalf virtually anything at all. Again, however, the attraction of such a mode needs to be understood. Perhaps, for many people, their assurance of safety depends on staying on the sidelines.[9]

We'll give fuller attention to these two variations a little later, when we consider the various factors bearing on the possibility of change.

Meanwhile, let's summarize: our willingness to expose our beliefs to disconfirming feedback may be considered to fall into three categories:

- A "most open" category, which is characterized by a searching attitude, by active curiosity, and by a positive (perhaps we can even say "fearless") receptivity. Hypotheses, and indeed incongruities, are sought, or if adventitiously encountered, seized upon. The mental attitude is one of security. Discrepancies are experienced as challenging, since they tease with the promise of a potential enlargement of one's world.

- An "intermediate" category, which is characterized by watchfulness, caution, and a testing attitude. Discrepancies are considered as evidence which needs to be attended to in order to develop a more satisfactory scheme for understanding.

- A "most closed" category, which is characterized by a conservative, protective attitude. Discrepancies are experienced as painful or nonsensical, since, if valued, they would threaten one's sense of being a continuously meaningful *effective* self.

It is perhaps redundant to say that for most of us, these levels of accessibility merge and shift in relation to one another almost continuously. They are best seen as rough categories only, useful to us as we attempt to discern order in what is in reality an ebbing, flowing, and swirling continuum.

We must also take note of our tendency in language to funnel such distinctions into moral categories of superiority/inferiority. "Above," "below," and, certainly, "superior" and "inferior" all have moral implications that may be entirely inappropriate. Clearly, to be human, we must have a set of assumptions upon which we can depend as we go about the normal business of our lives. Similarly, too, there are occasions when we don't have the time to appraise carefully all the conflicting evidence. And further, speculative, creative endeavor can be actively disruptive—indeed dangerous—if we are in the middle of urgently trying to get something done. Achieving the best balance of the different levels of openness in our lives is undoubtedly a fundamental and ever-continuing task of civilization. We must be particularly cautious, then, about the moral connotations of the words we use to describe how we distinguish *any* category of experience. "Open-mindedness," for example, is most frequently used as a eulogistic designation and "closed-mindedness" as a pejorative one. We need to remember, then, that, as Jerome Bruner puts it, "Constant open-mindedness equates to infinite distractability."[10]

Cautious we must be, but we can also transcend our tendency to settle too quickly upon judgmentally approving or disapproving characterizations. Indeed, we may on occasion be able to play creatively with the distinction between them. There is a wonderful characteristic anecdote that illustrates the quality of the relationship holding between Whitehead and Bertrand Russell when they were jointly working on the *Principia Mathematica*. Whitehead and Russell were apparently at odds about how to resolve a particularly difficult logical contradiction. "*You*, Bertie," exclaimed Whitehead in his exasperation, "are simple-minded, whereas *I* am muddle-headed!"[11] What a beautiful example of humane off-centeredness! (And a timely reminder, too, that the off-centered stance is *not a dispassionate one*.)

The balance of the levels of one's openness to experience undoubtedly varies throughout the stages of any human life, for it seems obvious that in early childhood the balance must favor a searching, engaged attitude, if only because there is no existing set of primary frame assumptions upon which to base one's expectations, and little ground in experience for the formulation of hypotheses. (Nor should we forget that early learning is subject to the limitations of a brain and nervous system that are still in the process of development.) This is a period of massive centricity, but also of great vulnerability to both physical and emotional context. Experiences that affirm the infant's subjective awareness of being effective enhance its exploratory activity.[12] Circumstances that suppress the opportunity for such affirmations curtail it. Successful exploration leads to not only physical but also emotional security. Both emotional security and physical security are essential for confidently engaging in the larger world of indirect (that is, symbolically mediated) experience.

A little later in life, it is the intermediate level that can be thought of as likely to be most salient, as—presuming the achievement of a fundamental emotional security—our search for both subjective meaning and objective sense become of central importance, and our aspirations for effectiveness in the world encourage our engagement with it. One is now expressing something that pushes beyond the continuity of one's inheritance. We could perhaps best describe it as the beginning of each individual's encounter with the possibility of contributing to the realization of the potential of humanity.

In later years, the balance shifts further. One's primary frame beliefs become solidified, and there are relatively few and circumscribed shiftings of the balance towards the more open levels. By this time, the available arena for new learning will have been determined by the fundamental assumptions about priority that had previously been set; the major decisions about where to place the emphasis in one's own life will tend to have been made, and we are usually more preoccupied with getting things done than with questioning what we are doing, or why. Any fortuitous discontinuity in one's life will nevertheless of course have the potential to shake up one's belief structure substantially, but much depends on whether our subjective experience of the meaning of such a discontinuity defines it as a disruption or an opportunity. We must take into account, too, that our commitment to a particular way of being can be such as to determine that an extreme disruption might have the power to shatter our very attachment to life itself.

It will probably also be apparent that whether our response to any event be engagement, withdrawal, defensiveness, or indifference will depend not only on what we have cumulatively come to believe, but also on the circumstances of the event, and, in particular, on whether or not the event transpired as a consequence of our pursuing some self-determined purpose. Since our feeling fulfilled depends on our sense of how effective we are in every aspect of our lives, clearly, our beliefs about our effectiveness are powerfully affected by whether what we have learned about life has been learned as a result of our own initiatives, or in spite of them. In particular, what is crucially affected is not only what we believe about ourselves as effective or ineffective agents of our own fulfillment, but also about others, depending on whether they are seen as facilitators or opponents of our efforts.

This is perhaps why it is that for a human being, both the defense of identity and the assertion of that identity can be as powerful an imperative for determining one's course of action as the instinct for survival is in other animals. To make one's own particular kind of sense of the world is, in fact, an assertion, an affirmation of one's own power as agent. It follows that for human beings, protection of continuity of meaning (that is, the particular meaning that, circumscribed as it may be, affirms the self as agent) can override concerns about purely physical survival. Whether or not it is sweet and proper to die for one's country, many of us have been willing to do so. To be willing to risk death, or actively to choose to die in order to assert or bear witness to our beliefs, is not only characteristic of saints or suicide-bombers. Any belief, however extreme, can be convincing if one's affirmation of self depends on it.

If, indeed, it is safe to assert that one's sense of effectiveness is crucial to one's feeling of personal worth, then human beings must have developed ways to compensate for the obvious fact that our efforts to control or accommodate to the enormous power Nature and circumstance have over our lives are relatively puny. The world is, in fact, recalcitrant; it kicks back. It doesn't always respond to us in the ways we would wish. The reality principle takes over in short order. We don't experience continued distress from knowing that if we fall off a high cliff we are unlikely to survive. We accommodate to these realistic physical restrictions upon our freedom of action in the early years of our lives, and concern ourselves with other types of opportunity. Symbolic processes give us plenty of alternatives.

The case is very different for restrictions of opportunity that we can attribute to the motives of others. We are clearly more likely to rage against the curbings of our effectiveness occasioned by other people than we are against those occasioned by physical circumstance. Physical circumstances are generically similar for all of us (notwithstanding, of course, any specific physical deficits or aberrations that reduce the size of any individual's total ambient). They do not, therefore, easily carry any implications of motivated hostility towards us. Modern civilizations have, for the most part, moved beyond attributing catastrophic natural events to the motives of gods who kill us for their sport. Social circumstances, however, can certainly carry implications of motivated hostility, since they can be attributed—sometimes accurately, sometimes mistakenly—to the self-serving motives of others. It is not surprising, then, that for people who judge themselves to be victimized by such processes, particularly in so far as their own freedom of action is concerned, the entire situation may be experienced as a threat to their very being.

In this latter case, it is probably fair to assert that centric concerns will become dominant. Symbolic processes will not be eschewed, but they will take a form that is analogous to the instinctive responses of animals confronted by physical danger. If other human beings are seen to behave towards us as if we were ourselves not fully human, and therefore not worthy of humane consideration, but rather as obstacles to be overcome, or resources to be exploited, we may find ample justification for ourselves adopting similar attitudes towards those we perceive as our oppressors. In all such circumstances, it seems that the de-humanizing of our opponents is the almost necessary prerequisite for our inhumane treatment of them. (Significantly, military training emphasizes from the outset the dehumanizing of the enemy.) The history of humankind, sadly, provides a multitude of examples, from the almost amusingly trivial to the utterly horrific.[13] The common factor in all is the suppression of any sense of fellowship. In the First World War, the upper échelons of command on both sides came down heavily on those who famously fraternized with "the enemy" on Christmas Day, sharing with one another photographs of their families.

The symbolic resources and opportunities available to us in these different sets of circumstance themselves seem to be of two distinct types. One offers the opportunity for an actual increase in real effectiveness. The other provides a serviceable but delusional substitute.

In the first type, as we have seen, we are enabled to enhance our realistic effectiveness by creating artifacts and procedures that expand the range of our perceptual and action ambients. Beyond those practical abilities, too, we have experienced a subtle but significant shift in the nature of our sensibility: we have become able to recognize that there are different orders of effectiveness than the one we experience as resulting from simple cause/effect physical action.

In particular, our symbolic abilities afford us the opportunity to transcend the realistic physical limitations of our situation through understanding.

Understanding vastly expands the range of our physical effectiveness. We can both perceive more about the world, and powerfully increase our ability to act upon it. The most significant attribute of understanding, however, is that it permits us the realization that we are not simply subject to the inexpressibly awesome power of the universe, but that we *direct our own future.*

Beyond understanding and its derivatives, moreover, there is the possibility of an even further realistic expansion of our effectiveness in the world. Symbolism invites us to enjoy our abilities by playing with them, not only to explore their creative possibilities, but also simply to experience the joy, the excitement, of exercising our imagination. Imaginative play is probably as important for the development of our minds as physical play in childhood is for the development of a healthy body. It is hard to express adequately in words the far-reaching effects of such activity. We can, of course, summarize its character by discerning that its processes are themselves not uncommonly a critical element in creative effort, and that they are most obviously apparent in the realm of art. After-the-fact analysis, however, scarcely does justice to the potential for new realizations and different kinds of understanding that is contained in such activity. Nor should we underestimate the courage that may be necessary fully to commit ourselves to them. To talk about such activities is clearly valuable, but insufficient. We have to honor what is required of us to *engage* in them.

The practical effects of artistic activity and, indeed, of play itself, may be difficult to discern, but it cannot be denied that their metaphoric, aesthetic, emotional, and elucidatory power can be such as to transform our lives. In the words of William Carlos Williams:

> It is difficult
> to get the news from poems
> yet men die miserably every day
> for lack
> of what is found there.[14]

Indeed, the different modes of action and consequent understanding born of science and art are manifestly important enough for them to require a fuller treatment than can be afforded here. Let's keep to our more immediate task, then, and move to the second major type of alternative action that symbolic processes make available to us.

This second type comprises some of the most powerful and influential determinants of human motive. It consists of various schemes of imagined reality that are taken as absolute and accurate representations of the way the world is. Such serviceable delusions have the power to entrain the dedicated belief and loyalty of vast numbers of people. They differ profoundly from the kind of imagined realities that are put forward as hypotheses about the world, since the latter are suggested as matters for empirical test, and can therefore yield to evidence that refutes them. Delusional schemes, in contrast, are undismayed by inconsistencies. Somewhere, somehow, there is postulated a higher, divine consciousness whose motives are scarcely accessible to us, and most certainly not to rational thought. Such schemes may perhaps be most accurately thought of as placebos for the pain many of us experience when we are unable to make overall sense of existence itself. We are particularly prone to embrace any explanatory system that promises peace of mind and reciprocal affirmation as the rewards for adherence to it. The attractions of companionship in wishful thinking are difficult to resist.

Indeed, the specific attraction of delusional schemes of imagined reality, their ability to entrain belief at the primary frame level, is that they offer the reassurance of a connection to the possibility of absolute understanding. Such schemes can thereby engage the passionate embrace of millions. They are serviceable, because they respond to the profound psychological need of human beings to feel effective in spite of the limitations of their own understanding. Warmed by the support of others, the adherents to such schemes disregard or consider irrelevant the practical and logical incongruities to which their beliefs give rise. Apologists may attempt to find rational arguments for their convictions, but the more frequently found justifications tend to treat rational processes for understanding as irrelevant. This is the so-called "leap of faith." To a theoretically objective external observer, the enormous variety of such schemes, each of them similar in their self-proclaimed superiority over other such schemes, itself constitutes the clearest evidence of their delusional character. Once one has rejected rationality, the number of possible irrational schemes is as endless as numbers themselves.

Unfortunately, the practical consequence of many such widely embraced primary frame beliefs is that they polarize humanity into believers and unbelievers, allies or enemies. We shall have occasion to investigate this phenomenon further, particularly with regard to its terrible consequences, but we first need to understand the psychological underpinnings of the search for such absolutes.

Daniel Essertier suggests a persuasive answer:

> Horror of doubt is natural to consciousness. Doubt is its supreme
> menace, for it threatens the keystone of the whole mental structure:
> the affirmation of self. In affirming anything, the mind affirms
> itself. And even further, it is for the sake of thus affirming itself
> that it makes any affirmation at all.[15]

A set of such affirmations can not only constitute the primary
frame assumptions of an individual, but (as many have discovered
to their cost over the course of human history) the primary frame
assumptions, and thus the identity, of a large group. In such a
case, the continuity of meaning of such a group will be attached
to such affirmations, and therefore attacks on the assumptions
will be experienced as threats to the very identity of the group.
Here is Langer's take on the phenomenon:

> We are no longer in the world-building stage of rampant imagination,
> when every person could indulge in the most extravagant fantasies
> and every invention passed for a reality; most civilized people
> today limit their categorical religious assertions to the affirmation
> of formally-stated tenets shared by a number of other persons.
> That number may be small—the membership of a deviant sect
> or even a secret cult—or immense, like that of the Roman Catholic
> Church, Islam, or Hinduism, each uniting millions. The passionate
> feeling with which we tend to profess our faith shows that, even
> in modern society the average person has a deep need of asserting
> the nature of his world, in order that he may constantly realize
> and confirm his own being.[16]

Unfortunately, there are many varieties of faith that are not
simply professed, but aggressively promoted. Nor are these beliefs
restricted to what we conventionally consider religious. Assertions
about the superiority of one's race, one's culture, one's gender,
one's politics, possibly even one's way of life, almost necessarily

result in the condemnation, vilification, and victimization of those who do not belong to the chosen group, or who offer alternative possibilities for belief. The process involved is dissociation. Moreover, the logical outcome of such activities is the dehumanizing of the alien group; and dehumanization, as we have previously argued, is the necessary prerequisite for treating such groups as not meriting humane conduct towards them. A group that can be characterized as both an "empire" and "evil" cannot thereby have any claim on our sympathy or our regard. Any possibility of fellow feeling is knowingly extinguished. Anyone who questions the validity of such absolute generalizations risks designation as a supporter of the vilified group, and is thus also dehumanized. This was particularly apparent in the United States in the aftermath of the events of September, 2001. The naming of such people varies, according to the nature of the belief structures that their behavior threatens: one may be called a traitor, a disciple of the devil, a pig, an apostate, a heretic, an anarchist. A variety of revolting attributes inevitably accompany such designations: "dirty," "unprincipled," "immoral," "self-serving," "unclean," "greasy," "cowardly," and so on. With sufficient repetition, what could logically be seen originally as a simple descriptive term may become indistinguishable from a clearly vilifying one. I was once present at a meeting to discuss international aid programs in which one participant argued against the sending of humanitarian aid to a particular country because "they're all communists." She might have as easily said, "They're all pagans ... They're all anti-Christs ... They're all homosexuals ... They're all savages ..." The specific terms matter less than their common character: they dissociate the vilified group from the community of humanity.

A primary frame belief that massively emphasizes centric preoccupations and concerns can clearly, *in extremis,* not only convincingly persuade a believer to die for it, but also foster the belief that it is justifiable to maim, torture, or kill other people in defense of it. If one's own survival is felt to be at stake—and for human beings, as we have shown, this equates to the survival of a strongly espoused identity—then all other motives may be overwhelmed.[17]

The major attraction of violence as a solution to conflicts about values is that the power to destroy gives, if only temporarily, the illusion of effectiveness: one is at least doing something that has a clearly visible, if transitory, result. It was the Canadian socialist Tommy Douglas, I believe, who pointed out that you can't kill an idea. Killing people who espouse an idea that one finds threatening can evidently appear a satisfactory alternative. If we can personify the idea of evil, for example, we can in consequence maintain the illusion that we can destroy it.[18]

To endeavor to dehumanize in order ultimately to destroy an opponent is simply one form of protective maneuver, albeit an extreme one. Maneuvers to protect continuity of belief will demand our close attention shortly, but we first have to further our understanding of the nature of error itself. If we can understand how errors happen, then we'll know what will be necessary to prevent them. If we can understand the circumstances that foster error, for example, then we'll know how to promote better kinds of circumstance. Further, and ultimately, if we can understand the ways in which erroneous representations of the world are protected, and protected specifically against normally corrective feedback, then we'll be able to discern how to interrupt, modify, or counter-balance those processes. These are the next items for our attention.

5

Error

GIVEN THE COMPLEX mix of instinct, genetic predisposition, pre-conceptual thought, conceptual representations, propositional thought, and individual experience that together make up the mental world of any human being, it is clear that our errors in perception, thinking, and action may be attributed not only to the individual workings of each of these elements but also to their interaction. To understand better the workings of the mix, it's helpful to consider the unique characteristics of each element (bearing in mind, too, the assumptions we may have already made about them).

It may be tempting to consider instinct as an outcome of the cumulative "learning"[1] of a particular species over its complete phylogenetic history, a learning that is currently represented genetically in every surviving life form. However, phylogenesis simply summarizes how evolutionary processes have enabled a species to survive. For species survival, errors by individuals are only important statistically, by whether or not they critically affect the likelihood that the rate of procreation matches or exceeds the rate of extinction. Instinct may be prone to error or inadequacy in individual circumstances, but if these circumstances are rare enough in the long term, then there is no sufficient cause for genetic modifications to become salient. I'm sure all of us, at times, have been startled by what we judge to be the relative "stupidity" of other creatures when confronted by a circumstance for which they were genetically unprepared. My own most memorable experience of this was when I came across an all-but-exhausted humming bird that was banging itself repeatedly against the closed glass window of a long-abandoned wilderness cabin. It was frantically trying to find a way out into the clear air beyond the window, and seemed to be totally unaware that the door through which it had entered the cabin in the first place was still open, and in fact offered its only possibility of exit. As outside observers of the propensity for such errors in other creatures, we may well be prone to a feeling of relative smugness about our own position: prone, that is, until we take stock of our own propensity to bang ourselves repeatedly against unperceived barriers of a less physical kind. Our instincts, too, can fail to meet the circumstances of the case. Does any other species consistently war against itself?

In fact, phylogenetic inheritance is clearly not directly *equivalent* to individual learning. Individual learning depends on being responsive to the difference between expectation and reality, and, by definition, it always results in a modification of some kind. It would be a step too far, however, to suggest that there is a species' equivalent to expectation. It *is* clear that threats to the survival of a species do, over generations, result in adaptive modifications both of form and of behavior, but it is difficult to think of genetic development itself as evidence of a species' intelligence, as some geneticists do.[2] The modifications brought about over the course of any species' genetic history simply summarize the manner in which the evolutionary process itself has successfully worked in that particular case. No individual decision-making is involved.

The learning that occurs in any individual lifespan, by contrast, in both the human and the non-human case, always requires the experiencing of an incongruity between what is anticipated or planned for and what actually occurs. In this respect, pre-conceptual learning and conceptual learning are similar. What is most importantly common to both, however, is that an unperceived or imperceptible circumstance can have no effect on the learning process, since no incongruity is registered. I am over-simplifying. In the human case, our conceptual abilities themselves allow for other possibilities. An event for which we do not have adequate—or indeed any—conceptual form, can nevertheless mistakenly be taken as an instance of an entirely different, readily available conceptual shape. Most of us probably have a distinctive style of such errors: that is, we will tend to have developed a characteristic habitual pattern of such error. If we are familiar with something, even if we do not fully understand it, we are less likely to pay attention to the incongruities to which it gives rise. Moreover, as Abraham Kaplan has pointed out,

> When we have related what is observed to our own experience, our curiosity is likely to be satisfied, and familiarity serves in the place of genuine explanation. We feel that we understand why someone did something when we see it as no more inexplicable than our own behavior . . . But we know why the someone did the something only in the psychological sense of 'for what purpose,' not in the scientific sense of 'for what reason'; in short, we apprehend motives, and not causes.[3]

Erroneous understanding of a familiar phenomenon is often illustrated in our use of a "junk-term"[4] of some kind to describe it: a pseudo-explanatory attribution, for example, like "crazy," or a cliché formula, like "You can't fight City Hall." Each illustrates the delusion that what is familiar is well understood; and, clearly, what is well understood does not require further investigation. As Magorah Maruyama expressed it, "People don't pay attention to problems they believe they have already solved."[5]

Perhaps the commonest kind of junk-term is one that classifies an experienced event or circumstance as "noise" and dismisses it as irrelevant. Disregarded phenomena may nevertheless turn out to be very relevant indeed. Practically, it might seem that there is no difference between a phenomenon that is apparently not registered at all, and one that is determined to be of no consequence. However, although disregarding noise may be equivalent to its not entering consciousness, the disregarded element may still be a factor in determining motive, and possibly even a critical one, as we'll see a little later.

In registering what is going on in its environment, the most important task for any creature is to determine whether it is facing a danger or an opportunity. Not surprisingly, any animal weighs its survival more importantly than any other factor. The consequence of not registering, or disregarding, the presence of a predatory hawk might well result in the demise of the inattentive mouse. The consequence of taking avoiding action when it is in fact unnecessary, is, by contrast, trivial. Needless avoidance action is much to be preferred to its alternative.

The situation is rather different for us symbol-using animals. As we have seen, survival for a human being may be geared to the survival of identity; that is, to continuity of belief, rather than to purely physical continuity. I am not suggesting that any human being would be unlikely to dodge a suddenly moving, apparently menacing shadow on a dark street, but rather that, if a fundamental assumption of their world-view was experienced as being under threat, they would be less concerned about physical consequences than symbolic ones.

In the human case, then, in the right circumstances, one might give more weight to the survival of an idea than to one's physical wellbeing, or even to physical survival itself. Nor should we forget that the continuity of belief being protected could well be the instrumental assumptions that underlie the kind of sense we make. We are unlikely to investigate such instrumental assumptions, as we have seen, as the powerful feelings aroused by our beliefs about value may have preempted any questioning about how we might have arrived at them. The propositions which themselves define our modes of evaluating experience will remain invisible. We'll investigate our various ploys to protect identity more fully in Chapter Seven.

In the human case, too, the risks envisaged in correcting a presumed error might well include the dismantling of the (possibly expensive) infrastructures to which the previous errors had given rise. These infrastructures, and the activities required for their maintenance, might well have "secondary gain" elements it would be costly to sacrifice or to modify. A bureaucracy built up around a particular set of assumptions about its role in serving some socially accepted purpose would undoubtedly be thrown into a crisis if the premises for its very existence were unequivocally revealed to be misguided. In other words, there could be institutional costs and a threat to particular continuities of meaning in the correction of former errors in such a case. The protection of continuity of identity of an institution, although it may involve somewhat different procedures, is nevertheless simply a larger case of the protection of personal cumulative meaning. Personal continuities of meaning can, in fact, be inexorably attached to institutional affiliations. For any of us, our sense of who we are is necessarily permeated with primary frame assumptions about the nature of our affiliations with others. A powerful—and appalling—example of the complex behaviors that can result is provided by the conduct of members of the Nixon Administration in relation to the U.S. Senate's Watergate hearings in 1973. A more topical example is provided by the behavior of the Roman Catholic Church in its response to the widespread evidence of sexual abuse of children by members of its priesthood.

Further, as we shall examine more fully later, how others discern and define the affiliations we are deemed to have can be a significant factor in determining their behavior towards us. Prejudicial definitions of who we are, on the basis of where we were born, what our physiological characteristics are, or what our sexual identity is, are widespread givens in the experience of most of us. Are we "black," or "white," or "yellow," or male, or female, or Irish, or Czech, or Serb, or Bosnian, or Han, or Tibetan, or . . .? The list of attendant available prejudices is endless.

There is yet a further critical difference in the human case. Since any symbolic system imposes an abstract representational structure on human experience, it squeezes that experience into a particular shape, one that is more amenable to mental manipulation, more in harmony with existing feeling, or, perhaps, is easier to incorporate into the already complex framework of a given person's understanding. All representational systems, therefore, are circumscribed as to their abilities. We can think of them, perhaps, as two-faced:

They permit, but they also exclude.

They facilitate, but they also inhibit.

They liberate, but they also restrict.

This situation presents a serious dilemma only if we fail to take account of it, and expect of any specific system what it cannot deliver, or assume that what it delivers is *necessarily* true to reality. Since we have a number of distinct symbolic systems, and extraordinary variance within their various forms, we always have the option of compensating for the limitations of any given form by exploring the possibilities afforded by another. Maps are a more immediately informative representation of geographic location than descriptive words; tidal graphs are more accessible to quick understanding than the columns of figures in tidal tables; histograms are more compelling to the viewer than numerical summaries of relative frequency over different time-periods; technical drawings (and now, of course, computer-generated graphics) are unmatched for revealing the complexities of physical structures yet to be realized.

In some cases, indeed, the translation into a different form of representation can open up a whole new realm of exploration and hypothesis. The ability to convert iterated fractal equations into visual form (a choice simply unavailable to mathematicians before the explosive growth of electronic computer ability in the last decades of the twentieth century) resulted not only in the colorful visual representations of the endless Mandelbrot set, but also in practical extrapolations that have transformed communications technology and data-retrieval systems throughout the world. In a way, in fact, we can perhaps think of our representational systems themselves as compensating for the limitations of the kind of pre-conceptual learning evidenced by other animals. Since we ourselves go through a pre-conceptual phase of learning in early childhood, and since the particulars of such learning tend to be invisible to us, it's important to try to understand better how that learning is actually achieved.

Pre-conceptual learning does result in an internal representation of some kind, as we have seen, but such representations can be understood rather as a kind of inventory of *signals*,[6] that is, of recognizable physical signs of certain kinds of phenomena that have previously been encountered, and which trigger responses that were successful in the past. What seems to be represented internally, then, is not a concept, but the recognition of a stimulus, and the memory of the feeling produced by it. Bruner has speculated that so-called stimulus-response theory gives an adequate description of the processes involved.[7] Any creature, including a human being, may be *conditioned* by a particular pattern of exposure to given events, and develop a characteristic pattern of response to them. The result of such conditioning determines the manner in which any creature chooses from its inventory of available responses, which is itself circumscribed, of course, by the limitations of that creature's action ambient. To an external observer, conditioned behaviors may be indistinguishable from those that stem from instinctual, reflexive action. The responses have become automatic.

Pre-conceptual learning has been summarized as having arisen from direct "empractic" and "eiconic" experience.[8] In other words, it is a consequence of one's physical interaction with the world and one's recognition of signs; that is, of identifiable visual, auditory, tactile, olfactory or gustatory experiences that are taken to be indicative of particular circumstances. Most importantly, although those experiences do bear on the perceiver's choice of action, they do *not* bear on understanding, since understanding requires the use of the deductively formulated propositions made possible by conceptual thinking.

To summarize, then: in human beings, instinctual responses derived from the genetic history of one's species are intermingled with the stimulus-response learning arrived at through individual pre-conceptual experience, and the propositional learning permitted by concept-definition. Let's try to find a way to organize more simply our knowledge of this complex mix. Our overall objective is to understand how we may arrive at the truest possible representation of the world: in short, how to make the best possible kind of sense of it. Ignorance may indeed be blissful, but it is a good program neither for survival nor for self-realization. It is true representations alone that optimize our adaptability, and thus the likelihood of our survival both individually and as a species. The realizing of individual potential is a necessary component of the process that in turn contributes to realizing the potential of our kind. To help us get closer to that desirable objective, then, let's look at the possible ways in which we can be mistaken in our efforts to make sense.

The possibilities seem to be as follows:

1. An event may be perceived incorrectly; that is to say, its content, its phenomenal presence, may be discerned incorrectly. (In ornithological studies, for example, a rapidly moving simulated hawk silhouette overhead was reacted to by the study sample of ducklings as if it were indeed a hawk, and not simply a piece of cardboard.)[9] As we saw earlier in the case of our hypothetical mouse, errors of this kind tend to result almost inevitably from the instinct to avoid danger.

(This is an error of perception.)

2. An event may be registered as being a sign of some particular thing, when in reality it is a sign of some other kind of thing. In the case of the fabled dog in Aesop's story, the reflection of a piece of meat was the sign of a pool of water, not another meal. In research on various types of bird behavior, it is well established that, in some species, individuals will attack their own image in a mirror.[10] Phylogenetic inheritance has in many species responded to these characteristic types of error by fostering the circumstances in which other creatures can be tricked into making them. Genetically engineered camouflage is widely found in the natural world, as is deceptive activity contributing to predatory effectiveness. Many creatures are known to have, over generations, evolved protective coloration that enhances their probability of survival. Others have evolved the ability to set traps for other creatures that depend on the other creature's being deceived as to the significance of what its senses detect. These practical deceptions, which, remarkably, are specifically fitted to the perceptual and action ambients of other animals, are not always specifically significant for creatures of other species. Male cuttlefish, for example, can take on the coloration of a female when attempting to copulate with a female, a phenomenon that must well be confusing to the competition. When it comes to human deception, however, the advantages afforded by the versatile resources of derivative symbolism enable us to extend the repertoire of our deceptive activity far beyond the limits determined for other animals by the restrictions of their genetic endowment.

3. An event or circumstance may be appraised as having relevance to the protagonist animal when it has no such relevance. (Orchids have developed blossoms that suggest

to amorous wasps that the orchid is a female ready for intercourse. This is of no use to the wasps, but it is what enables the flower to disseminate its pollen.)

4. An event or circumstance may be appraised as having no relevance when it in fact does. (Our anthropocentrism may lead us to believe that "many a flower is born to blush unseen, and waste its sweetness on the desert air"[11] but flowers don't blush in order to satisfy the aesthetic cravings of human beings. The sweetness of flowers is essential to their success in attracting the pollinating insects that enable them to propagate.)

5. An event or circumstance may be thought to have positive significance when it in fact has a negative significance. That is, dangerous events or circumstances may be registered as being harmless, or even of benefit. Frogs are attracted to the insects trapped by the nectar of the carnivorous pitcher plant, in some cases fatally.

6. An event or circumstance may be appraised as having dangerous significance when it in fact has positive or neutral significance: a far less significant error, of course, than its opposite.

(These are errors of judgment.)

7. The protagonist may engage with an event when it is unsafe, or useless, to do so.

8. The protagonist may avoid or flee from an event when it would have been safer, or more productive, to engage.

9. The protagonist may, through uncertainty, critically delay action.

(These are errors of action, and follow naturally from prior errors of perception or of judgment. Errors of perception or of judgment are nevertheless only apparent to an outside observer through their derivatives in action. Any observer, of course, may also be deceived as to what is actually happening, and thus may be mistaken as to the nature of the error, or indeed as to whether an error has in fact been made.)

What kinds of errors result from the ability to conceptualize? I'll simply add them to the list.

10. The concept can be formed in error. The concept thus formed can not only "seduce" data to its own parameters, but may also, through the propositions it fosters, determine the moral attitude of the protagonist. These strictures consequently curtail the effectiveness of dialectical methods for reconciling different points of view in order to arrive at truth. In argument, protagonist and antagonist alike can be deceived as to the meaning of the terms they are using. How often do we find after periods of protracted and sometimes belligerent disagreement that we were unknowingly assigning different meanings to critically important words?

Transient erroneous conceptual definition occurs almost inevitably in the years of childhood.[12] As one's familiarity with the resources of symbolic processes increases, however, these early stumblings are for the most part quickly superseded, at least with regard to physical phenomena. It is clear, however, that, for all of us, there remain pockets of inadequate conceptualization. These will not always be readily apparent to an observer or interlocutor. The inadequacy of such conceptualizations may reveal itself only in incongruities between apparent understanding and consequent action. Conversation alone is unlikely to reveal inadequate formulations, as faulty abstraction does not readily exhibit itself, particularly when conventional words are being used in conventional circumstances.

11. No satisfactory conceptualization yet exists for a phenomenon that manifests itself but is not registered as having a coherent independent identity. In such cases, no knowledgeable proposition can be formulated upon which to base any future action. It is significant that there is no word for "obey" in Inuktitut. The legal niceties important to the immigrant colonizers from Europe had little meaning for the Inuit of Canada's far north. For the new immigrants, creating new-junk terms and cliché formulas to cope with their failure to understand the native cultures was probably virtually inevitable.

12. Relationships between the various elements of experience may be incorrectly understood because of faulty use of a sound explanatory system. Linguistic logic, for example, applies specifically to language, and not necessarily to reality.[13] The long debate over the exact nature of light was a direct result of our being unable to accept that it could "be" both a wave and a particle. Similarly, although "Are you for us, or against us?" is recognized in logic as excluding the possibility of a more complex middle ground, it is so widely used as a ploy in argument (it is, of course, a rhetorical device) that we should consider the possibility that the tendency to polarity that it illustrates is due to the working of a different *kind* of logic. It seems likely that the root discrimination of this form of logic derives from the very earliest of distinctions, that made between what is within and what is without, that is, between what is felt to be self and what is felt to be other. The implications of this distinction are far-reaching, and will demand our closer attention shortly.

13. Since different articulate systems of symbols exist, both within cultures and between them, there is the very real possibility that we will misunderstand the symbols other people are using when attempting to communicate with us. Critical connotative differences in language can easily escape literal translation.

    Of particular importance is that, since symbolic systems differ in their ability to represent effectively, translation across symbolic systems risks erroneous substitution, or even loss of essential information, and thus vitiates meaning. Some systems cannot accommodate meanings that others romp around in. "If I could explain it," Isadora Duncan is reputed to have said after one of her performances, "I wouldn't have needed to dance it." That Duncan did feel the need to dance it supports the contention that some forms of experience cannot be adequately translated. If this were not true, it is hard to believe that we would have any kind of art at all.

14. Messages carried by means of symbols can be deliberately formulated to deceive. Where deception serves the needs of truth, as in poetic, or other aesthetic systems ("All art is a lie," said Picasso), it can be justified as moral purpose, but in the context of a discursive system ostensibly used dialectically (that is, in expectation of the same kind of ineluctable feedback as is afforded us in the physical realm), willful deceptions inhibit the discovery of truth.

    Unfortunately, the commitment to truth, rather than to deception, cannot be assumed, even of those who are ostensibly utterly committed to it. Scientists who have deliberately falsified research findings are unfaithful to their responsibilities to humankind. We are by dint of experience more likely to be attuned to the deceptions of politicians and of advertisers, of course, but all who deliberately misrepresent reality to others in order to achieve a singularly personal advantage are nevertheless placing obstacles in the path of our evolution towards a more humane world.[14]

The use of symbols actively to deceive means that the discernment of meaning in the symbolic arena is plagued by the very difficulty whose absence in the purely physical domain was so vividly remarked upon by Einstein. Einstein, it will be remembered, noted that God (i.e., Nature) might be subtle, but certainly not malicious.[15] In the realm of symbolic communication we may, by dint of positive experiences with our interlocutors, come to trust them, *but there will be occasions when we are mistaken.* The motives for deception may not be vicious, but we can by no means assume that, because Nature does not set out to deceive us, neither will people. Indeed, since we human beings only awaken to the significance of the social factor in the matrix in which we live our lives at a relatively late point, when we have already absorbed most of the basic assumptions, formal as well as psychological, of the culture in which we were brought up, we may be totally unaware of the errors passed on to us, advertently or inadvertently, before we had the ability to assess any experience critically. Discerning that others might have deceptive motives, or discovering that our interlocutors might themselves be deceived, comes only with the development of off-centered awareness.

15. The way of thinking fostered by a particular system of symbols is inappropriately applied to a field beyond that in which it originally established its explanatory or evocative power, or to problems for which it is unsuited. "Some of the major disasters of mankind have been produced by the narrowness of men with a good methodology," said Whitehead.[16] We may extend this variant with some justice to what Kaplan calls "the law of the instrument." The law of the instrument takes many forms, the simplest of which provided Kaplan's prototype case:

"If you give a little boy a hammer, everything he encounters will turn out to need pounding."[17]

Burke summarized it in "moral" terms:

"The pugilist will ethicize his fists."[18]

Ursula Franklin emphasized the practical consequences:

"Any task is structured by the available tools."[19]

In fact, the simple availability of tools, and indeed terms, may have as much to do with their use as any discriminating mental preference. The availability or unavailability of either can have profound effects, both on what one does and how one does it. Terms may have far-reaching pragmatic implications, and tools may have powerful psychological ones. The poet Robert Bringhurst tellingly observed that the perceived beauty of weapons is a significant factor in our decision to use them.[20]

Of particular significance to us in our everyday lives, then, is not simply the narrowness of a particular method, but also the restrictions imposed by the conscious or unconscious promotion of a particular mode of thought, by reason of the terms—including metaphorical ones—that set the shape of our mental representations. Not only can such terms promote a specific, circumscribed *image* that can hold us to a colonizing idea that diminishes our ability to discern critical differences in experience, but they can also present a restricted *model* of how things work. Many cultures are at the moment rife with language derived from the vocabularies of conflict, and of sales. In consequence, "success," and the manner of achieving it, tends to be seen as necessarily involving the defeat of a competitor, or the possession of more things. The effects of these attitudes can be subtle, but nevertheless critical in their influence on the way we think, and therefore on the way we act. The resources of metaphor are many, however, and powerful metaphors can have profound corrective implications. I personally find it helpful to think of the control of preferred vocabularies as akin to a "colonizing" procedure that establishes narrow "empires" of thought, each of which serves the centric interests of particular groups. To determine the vocabulary for representing and discussing human affairs gives any group, whether it be an oligarchy, a nation, a religion, an ethnic group, a gang, an institution (in short, any organized group whatsoever) a powerful position in relation to its own interests. The choice or refutation of a particular vocabulary can be a powerful political act, since it promotes or refutes a particular organizing image of reality itself.[21]

My own choice of metaphor, of course, illustrates the point. It's important to emphasize, then, as inevitably the reader will discover for the thinking and argument used in this book, that no thinker, even the most profound, is immune to the tendency to error arising from the preference for analyzing and attempting to solve problems in the terms, and through the procedures, he or she has come to trust, and with which either one feels most familiar. Being alert to the possibility of this kind of error can certainly help us avoid the most blatant pieces of narrow-mindedness, and there are also more systematic corrective measures to be discussed later, but no individual measure will itself *infallibly* result in our being free of this kind of error; for much of what we believe, and particularly what we believe about how to think, is outside our awareness.

16. There is an aesthetic satisfaction in realizing the full potential of any symbolic form, that is, in following its "syntax" through to a "logical" conclusion.[22] This kind of pursuit appeals for its own sake, regardless of any mediating function. An unresolved melody causes us an aesthetic frustration that is

akin to our uneasiness in allowing a sentence to remain incomplete. One can follow a thought through to an invalid conclusion, simply on the basis of its satisfying syntactic structure. We may also, indeed, find ourselves uneasy at a valid completion if its form is irritating to us. I remember one of my professors many years ago pointing out that an injunction, frequently displayed on public transit vehicles in England, cried out for some aesthetic modification. "Coughs and sneezes spread diseases" would be much more persuasive if it was not completed by "Trap the germs in your handkerchief" but by "Trap the germs in your handkerchieveses!"[23] It seems in fact that new discoveries in science, and new insights in art, often derive from playing with ideas and forms along such aesthetic lines, since aesthetic form itself seems to betoken an intuition of coherence and harmony less accessible to other methods of apprehension. It is perhaps this insight that led Langer to suggest that artistic forms are implicit, in that it is their structure which itself contains their content. That is, their significance is neither denotative nor specifically referential, even though their form may contain elements of both.[24]

17. In particular psychological circumstances, there seems to be a tendency for human beings to make affirmations without any supporting evidence. Possibly, this is because uncertainty makes resolute action almost impossible. In the history of humankind, the evolution towards off-centered awareness has been halting and hesitant. The primitive beliefs that led early humans to endow all kinds of physical entities with the attributes of human beings are no longer widely found today, but their residues seem to lurk in unexpected pockets even now. Stressful circumstances will often trigger the most unexpected jumps into primitive thinking.

Probably the most widely found manifestation of such primitiveness is in the attribution of motive. Fate or "the gods" are against us. Or, on the other hand, fortune must favor us, "because our cause is just." In argument, attributing hostile motives to one's interlocutor is also characteristic. The psychological underpinnings of such attitudes are of fundamental importance, and will require our more systematic attention shortly.

18. An event may be attributed to the non-symbolic realm when in fact it carries a symbolic significance. That is, it is assessed as unmediated, and thus carries no intended message. (A mariner marooned on a wilderness shore desperately attempts to signal for help to a distant vessel. The flash of light seen from her mirror is registered by the crew of the passing boat as a random reflection from the waves.)

19. An event may be seen as carrying mediated significance when it simply belongs to the non-symbolic realm. That is, we erroneously attribute a "message" significance to it, when there is in fact none. Auguries, the "reading" of tea leaves, the casting of horoscopes, and examples of the sympathetic fallacy belong in this group. (As, however, does the possibility that the crew of a boat will investigate a random flashing from the waves, believing it to originate rather from someone's emergency signal.)

Well, I've probably left out some variants, but this is still a pretty daunting list. This might be a good moment, then, to remind ourselves of Burke's comforting assurance that the freedom to err, notably occasioned by the complexities of symbolic representation, is simply the other side of the freedom to be right.[25] It is true that humankind has been proven right often enough for us to have brought about the enormous expansions of our ambient we've been discussing, but it must be faced that the possibilities for error arising out of the characteristics of derived symbolizations are such as to make it likely, and, indeed, inevitable, that all of us will to some degree inhabit representational worlds that are false. Thus:

Anyone living according to faulty propositions is to some degree living in a spurious "reality."

The fact that all human beings in various degrees do live in such spurious realities should not distract us from noticing that extensive spurious realities can create all kinds of problems, both for those who live in them, and those they affect. The most significant effect is the disruption and distortion of the feedback process upon which depends our ability to learn from experience. It is not extravagant to suggest that some people (and all people, to some degree) live in conceptual, and thus propositional, museums. In some cases, these museum-attitudes are enshrined in our social institutions. Indeed, it can be argued that any institutionalized mode of thought—whether or not it is also realized in some actual corporate structure—will quickly take on the character of a primary frame assumption, and consequently prove resistant to feedback that is incongruent with it.

We are faced, then, with at least three kinds of arena in which closed-mindedness exhibits itself. There is the closed-mindedness of individuals, there is the closed-mindedness of a particular mode of thought, shared by many, and there is the closed-mindedness that is incorporated into institutional social structures. All "institutionalized" thinking, whether of an individual, a variety of individuals, or a corporate structure, will thus be liable to show similar resistance to disconfirming feedback.[26]

In order to characterize the sphere of perception, proposition, and action that results when a pervasive frame is upheld in the face of massive contrary evidence, I shall use the phrase "virtual world."

To a theoretically objective observer, such persistent distortions of reality impress primarily, perhaps, because their rigidity closes us off from the abundant possibilities inherent in more accurate formulations. It is always tragic when human potential is dammed up in such fashion, because we are all the poorer for it. What is not as immediately registered, however, is that all such aberrations, including those espoused collectively, have their origin in an individual's sense of personal vulnerability, the fear of loss of significant personal continuity of identity, that is, of self-perceived continuous "meaningfulness."

How does an observer manage to discern whether any kind of error has occurred? Clearly, only by its consequences, which are revealed in incongruities. Just as we need to be aware of incongruities if we are to expand our knowledge of reality, so, too, do we need to take stock of what is incongruent in our own behavior if we are to entertain the idea of changing ourselves.

As we have seen, however, whether or not a protagonist can be aware of incongruity largely depends on whether or not an important element in that person's primary frame beliefs is being threatened. To an observer who is unaware of, or unable to decipher the sense of identity that may be under threat, or indeed unable to discern whether such a threat is in fact present, any attempt to produce a change in the situation may be based on completely mistaken premises. Moreover, since errors can occur without the involvement of a threat to identity, a threat to identity can only be confidently inferred if the interests of a protagonist are accurately known (that is, if we correctly know what purpose is guiding his or her activity) and all other circumstances for the accurate perception and cognition of an event are favorable— indeed, optimal. Given an accurate understanding of a person's interests, it is only when optimal circumstances for perception, thinking, and action exist that the presence of particular behaviors can be confidently attributed to the desire to protect identity. In the normal untidiness of everyday life, it is rarely possible to discern with certainty the true state of such circumstances, particularly since our access to knowledge of them may be restricted to indirect experience (for example, by listening to what other people have told us). Nevertheless, concentrating our attention upon such circumstances can often clear up misapprehensions.

This is the next item on our agenda.

6

Optimizing Opportunity

FOR MANY OF US, "optimizing opportunity" will probably register as a rather pompous title for what, in fact, will simply amount to a listing of conditions that we all feel we know so well that examining them at all seems a waste of time. However, in the interest of completeness, let's undertake at least a cursory inventory.

To summarize: we are about to investigate the optimal conditions for identifying, appraising, and dealing with differences between what we expect in our encounters with the world, and what we actually experience. These conditions may be characterized as environmental, circumstantial, psychological, or physical. Some conditions may apply only in the physiological realm, that is, the realm of direct experience; others may apply only in the conceptual realm, the realm of indirect experience. Notwithstanding this, it is important to note that conditions applying in the physical realm will often provide the metaphorical prototype for those that apply in the realm of the symbolic. "Lynxes towards others, moles towards ourselves," proclaimed La Fontaine, but he wasn't simply referring to eyesight.[1] In listing optimal conditions, then, it's good to be alert also to their metaphorical implications. These will not necessarily take a poetic form, although many may recall for us the aphorisms we find displayed, perhaps with a page of their own, in gift-calendars and "inspirational" books, the kind of statements, in fact, which at their best can cause us spontaneously to remark "How true!" before we instantly file them away in our minds as clichés or truisms that serve no immediate purpose. (I hope the following more systematic presentation will not share that rather unsatisfactory fate.)

With regard to the perceptual ambient, true perceptions probably require:

– A mature perceptual apparatus (i.e., we are concerned with theoretically "adult" perceivers). Mature perceptual ability, of course, does not itself guarantee error-free perception, any more than do any of the following.

– A complete perceptual apparatus (i.e., there is no deficit in sense abilities, as for example in blindness, short-sightedness, deafness, or other similar conditions).

– A healthy perceptual apparatus (i.e., there is no ear infection, eye irritation, or other transitory curtailing condition for any of the senses).

– Sufficient attention (one is focused on what is going on; it is now well established that using one's cellular telephone while driving is a significant factor in many automobile accidents).

– Sufficient contrast (for example, it isn't too dark to see clearly; sounds are sufficiently distinguishable from one another, and so on).

– Sufficient volume or intensity in relation to noise (the sound of traffic doesn't prevent you from hearing what your companion is saying).

– Sufficient time for an event to register. Von Uexküll, for example, noted that, as we age, our ability to register fast-occurring events diminishes substantially.[2] Older people tend to drive their cars more slowly because they experience their speed as greater than it "is" for young people. In his later years, the composer Igor Stravinsky movingly remarked that he didn't "have time to be in a hurry" any longer.

- Sufficient immediacy or proximity (i.e., one is close enough to see, or an event resulting from a prior cause is closely enough linked in time for the relationship to be apparent; long-delayed outcomes are difficult to trace back to an irrefutable cause).

- Opportunity to shift and compare different "viewing positions." (European explorers of Everest were initially confused as to the identity of the mountain when it was seen from different perspectives because Sherpas from different localities around the mountain, seeing it only from their own perspective, had given it different names.)

- Absence of repetitive exposure. (A background noise ceases to penetrate awareness after prolonged exposure to it; one momentarily "hears" one's refrigerator's compressor at the moment that it stops.)

- Absence of fatigue.

- Training or experience that has increased one's discriminatory abilities. (The trained or experienced bird-watcher will "see" more kinds of birds than a neophyte; the air-traffic controller will detect specific information on the radar screen that is incomprehensible to the visitor to the control tower; the medical doctor will be more alert to the significance of physical symptoms than would a lay person.)

- Freedom from stress or other distracting circumstance, such as would be constituted, for example, by a toothache (even philosophers are vulnerable), a fear of the consequences of error (for example in an examination), or by confidence-sapping self-criticism.

With regard to the symbolic ambient, optimal conditions for valid appraisal of incongruity would seem to consist of:

– Adequate intelligence (i.e., an adequate neuronal apparatus).

– A "true" conceptual scheme, or one whose errors are irrelevant to the situation at issue, and whose internal organization is such that it would be unlikely to be overwhelmed by large amounts of data.

– Adequate knowledge of, and familiarity with, the internal logic of the symbolic scheme in use (i.e., communications are in the same "language").

– Absence of stress, or fatigue, as above.

In the area of the action ambient, optimal opportunity for dealing with incongruity would require:

– A mature action apparatus (i.e., for symbolic, as well as physical action).

– A complete action apparatus.

– A healthy action apparatus.

– The requisite trained perceptual or executive skill to deal with specific circumstances. (Some people are unable to drive cars; few of us are able to pilot aircraft; even fewer are capable of undertaking a mission in space; there are, in fact, many areas of human activity that are closed to those of us without specialized expertise.)

– Being in a position to act.

– Being free to act.

– Supporting (rather than hostile or unfavorable) external circumstances.

Obviously, optimal conditions for perception, thinking, and action cannot automatically be assumed. Frequently, in everyday life, conditions are *not* optimal, and yet action can rarely be deferred until everything is as we should like it to be. Indeed, for many people, significant restrictions of their perceptual, conceptual, and action ambients are givens of their life-situation. We all, in effect, do the best we can. The givens of our individual life situations, however, may have become so familiar that they are unlikely to impinge upon our awareness with the same vividness as a new circumstance, and so, naturally, we tend to pay less attention to them. Making such constraints available to consideration could be a necessary first step in actually preventing error. (I have myself recently begun to lose hearing acuity. Even as my family and I attempted to deal with this circumstance, our misunderstandings increased substantially. A hearing aid belatedly but effectively resolved the situation.)

In the purely physical arena, fostering optimal conditions might, indeed, be relatively easy to achieve: turning on the light if it was too dark to see clearly; finding one's correct spectacles to read a book; turning up the volume on the radio; making sure that one was well rested before undertaking a difficult task; and so on. Even in the mediated arena, many improvements could easily be made: having a dictionary to hand while reading a foreign-language text, for example; or arranging for a delay before taking a major decision, in order to give more time for collecting relevant information, for considering alternative possibilities, or for simply getting a good night's sleep in order to

Making Sense of Us

return to the situation, refreshed, in the morning. Under the pressure of everyday events, I suspect we neglect such alternatives more frequently than we might think.

In the mediated arena, the significant difficulty arising for us is that we may be actively misled, as we have seen, either by the errors to which our representational systems are prone, or by conscious attempts by our interlocutors to deceive us. In such cases, obviously, the identification of an absence of optimal circumstances, and thus the ability to remove adverse conditions or substitute more favorable ones would be no simple matter.

Nevertheless, in spite of difficulties, the fostering of more propitious circumstances would, other things being equal, decrease the likelihood of error. That is, it would aid in the prevention of error in the first place. *This in itself would thus be a viable objective for humankind.* Alone, however, it would probably be insufficient to counter the attachment to persistent, already-committed error that is characteristic of our protection of a particular identity-continuity. Since a major task for humanity is to change what we persistently get wrong, we obviously need to achieve a more precise understanding of how we protect ourselves from being aware of our mistaken beliefs. This will provide the content of our next chapter.

90

7

Safeguarding Identity

PROTECTING ONESELF against a threat to one's identity clearly requires, at some level of mental activity, both a discrimination of what specifically needs to be protected, and also a choice of ways to do so most effectively. Neither decision may be a conscious one.

The more public aspects of one's identity, and how it is both sustained and expressed through one's active relationships with others, will occupy us shortly. Whether we feel a need to protect ourselves is undoubtedly affected by the affirmations, challenges, opportunities, or constraints afforded by those relationships. How we protect depends on our repertoire of action possibilities. This repertoire consists not simply of our physical abilities, but also of the terms, tools, procedures, and skills available to us. Regardless, however, of the presence or absence of conscious awareness on the part of any of us in protecting a given continuity of belief, it is important to remain keenly aware that a threat to one's identity can be experienced as powerfully as a threat to physical survival. A powerful threat to identity may, in short, enable centric preoccupations to preempt an alert consideration of the total context.

Many levels of mind are involved in the experiencing and appraising of an event, and neuronal decisions occur cumulatively before reaching consciousness. Tests of galvanic skin response in a variety of people have shown that there can be an emotional reaction to purely symbolic events prior to any subjective awareness.[1]

There can thus be an instinctive response to danger even before there is any conscious discrimination of what that danger is. We know from the work of Paul McClean[2] and his associates that the rhinencephalon (the "reptilian brain") and the limbic system of the brain can easily outpace the more complex processes of decision-making that are characteristic of the neocortex. All of us will flinch if someone even pretends to punch us in the eye. It may be startling, but certainly not offensive to logic, to discover that an apparently instinctive defense against danger in the physical realm has its counterpart in the conceptual. It does, however, appear to be contrary to the whole thrust of evolution itself that, in one study, the response of research subjects to the symbolic threat represented by *subliminally* presented unpleasant *words* was "to delay or even distort [perception of] them." (A kind of symbolic flinch, perhaps?) Evidently, in response to even subliminally registered symbolic threat, we can attempt to negate the very existence of the danger.

Could this be a critical issue for us in our own evolution, that the development of symbolic representations can in certain circumstances diminish our ability to identify true danger, simply because our apprehension of that danger is mediated by our symbols rather than registered without symbolic mediation?

It is scarcely surprising that an individual's subliminal awareness of threat should be difficult for an observer or an interlocutor to detect; difficult, perhaps, but not totally impossible. We may not in everyday life be able to detect variations in galvanic skin responses, but we can certainly be attuned to incongruities of visible behavior that "leak" evidence that a defense against threat is being mounted.

Our ability to detect such leakage can be substantially improved by training ourselves to pay more specific attention to certain previously disregarded aspects of physical demeanor and behavior, as has been convincingly demonstrated by Alexander Lowen[3] and by Paul Ekman, Wallace Friesen, and their associates.[4] Nevertheless, it is not surprising, given all the deceptive options available, that it is difficult for us to detect with precision whether any protagonist is feeling at risk. It might be thought that protective *activity* would be readily visible, but this is not always the case. In short, since any protagonist's *conscious* awareness of threat may, of course, become an important factor in his or her being able to examine and re-appraise the evidence, anyone hoping to help the protagonist come to a better understanding of the situation has to be pretty darned sure that *something is being protected*, since their own attempts to help might easily themselves be considered threatening.

In discriminating whether a threat is in fact present, we have to recognize the important role that habit and familiarity play in our experiencing of the world. They facilitate an economical use of our energies, steering us away from distractions. We classify experiences according to our appraisal of their specific meanings and file them away for reference or retrieval as needed. We filter our subsequent perceptions and cognitions in the light of those classifications, and usually without conscious awareness. In order to investigate how specific protective maneuvers work, then, it is important to distinguish them from these economizing procedures.

Protective activities, although they may formally resemble energy-conserving habit, may be thought hypothetically (by contrast) to require extra mental energy. They are specifically protective, rather than economizing procedures. Since their form is similar, however, an observer will initially have difficulty in distinguishing which is operative in a particular case. The most obvious difference between economizing procedures and those that specifically indicate a threat to identity is that the latter will show a persistent pattern of suppression of awareness of disconfirming feedback. Even this distinction may not be easily discerned, however, since habit itself necessarily results in a withdrawal of one's attention from those aspects of the environment considered to be irrelevant to the task at hand.

What might also lead an observer to diagnose inaccurately whether or not protective procedures are being used is the protagonist's direction of interest, and therefore of attention. A protagonist's apparent neglecting to give weight to incongruities in a situation, or to unexpected consequences of actions, may not only be attributable to less than optimal perceptual or cognitive conditions, but also to the particular specialized focus of that person's interest. A mind that appears closed may simply be directing its attention to some other matter, considered to be of more immediate importance. If an observer does not know what the protagonist's interests are, he or she is hardly well placed to judge what is really going on. We may, of course, not simply be ignorant of another person's interests; we may be actively mistaken about them. If, in contrast, we can "read" correctly the leaked evidence of another person's interests and concerns, we can be better placed to understand their behavior.

Abraham Kaplan tells a lovely anecdote reported originally by the famous chess-player Emanuel Lasker, in which Lasker recalled playing an exhibition match with another grand master on an oversize chess board on which the pieces were represented by people attired in the appropriate costumes. Lasker determined quite early that his opponent was prepared to take significant risks to preserve the white queen. Lasker used this knowledge to help him win the match. What was going on? Apparently the other grand master was very taken by the woman attired as his queen, and hoped to be able to make better acquaintance with her when the match was over. He would not be able to do this if the queen were taken, because she would then have simply left. Well, Lasker won the match, but his opponent's queen remained until the end, so perhaps his opponent can also be considered to have been successful in achieving his purpose. In the greater scheme of things he might even have considered himself the more successful. What if the young lady turned out to be the love of his life?

So, yes; we can be mistaken about the interests of others. What is less obvious is that we may as easily be mistaken about our own. Since our appraisal of the interests of others is inevitably influenced by the nature of our own interests, and particularly by the values that direct them, we would do well to be cautious about leaping to quick judgment. Any person's interests (including our own) will, of course, be experienced by that person as "making sense," even if, as Jon Elster has pointed out, a person's interests may not be to their interest.[5] Indeed, the interest of humanity itself may not be well served by its interests, particularly when so many of those interests compete or are at cross-purposes with one another. The apparent meaning of an act to the actor may be quite different from the meaning of that act to an observer whose position permits a wider understanding of the act *in its context*, and of the nature of the act as a subsidiary in a larger action process.

*Subjectively, in the absence of off-centered awareness, any person's interests—**including ours**—are likely to be experienced by that person with all the persuasiveness and all the apparent self-evidence that are characteristic of animal centricity.*

There is a particular case of the persuasiveness of interest that requires identifying in its own right. It is a class whose ramifications may frequently lie not only beyond an observer's ken, but beyond the protagonist's also. The communications theorist D. M. McKay has pointed out that the internal representations of any person include his or her cognitive and executive skills.[6] A significant aspect of such skills is that they lead to a specialized kind of attention. McKay calls this "feed-forward." Feed-forward refers to the influence of skills on the kind of attention given to new experience, an attention that affects the very nature of what is perceived and evaluated prior to engaging in action. Exposed to the same phenomenon, the skilled and the unskilled participant will experience different realities. Feed-forward, then, steers a protagonist's attention and activity, but only in accordance with the direction of that person's predetermined purpose. It specifically determines what that protagonist defines as noise and what as message. To one who is not privy to the system of understanding that is guiding the activity, the selective attention and behavior that stem from feed-forward may be indistinguishable from those stemming from protective motives.

There is quite a dilemma here, both for the person with a specific expertise, and for an outside observer. Not only may an observer fail to understand what the protagonist is doing, and why, but the protagonist will tend to disregard the qualifications of any potential observer to offer any kind of critical evaluation.

It is for this very good reason that we must be careful not too quickly to disqualify ourselves from questioning the consequences of specialized activity, including our own. We, too, can become unknowingly trapped inside a particular instrumentality, as "the law of the instrument" suggests. Most importantly, any person with specialized interests or skills may fail to take account of the "side-effects" of their particular specialization. Since I myself have only recently become aware of an error in my own appraisal of the world that undoubtedly affected my own effectiveness over many years, I hope I may be excused for suggesting that a greater humility about the possibility of our own proneness to error might well be a good thing.

The advantages of skilled specializations are thus almost necessarily linked to their disadvantages. The positive effects, as the negative ones, are readily apparent. On the one hand, potential distractions can be excluded; on the other, what is excluded from attention may not only vitiate both process and outcome, but also prove devastatingly harmful in a larger context. In spite of its downside, however, we must take special note that it is specialization of attention and activity that has permitted human beings to bring about the most extraordinary advances in both understanding and achievement. It is hard to believe that any of the significant achievements of humankind could have been brought about without such specialized attention and action. It is in full awareness of this context, then, that we nevertheless remark that feed-forward is itself simply a specialized kind of attitude, and a given habitual attitude inevitably contains assumptions about continuity of meaning, and therefore of identity.

Inner representations of skill, however, cannot be considered to have the same kind of status in one's mind as beliefs, since the representation of a particular skill in one's neuronal network is not vulnerable in the same way that beliefs are. Some skills are mental, and don't require any special motor ability, but others, obviously, involve complex muscle coordination and control. Clearly, we cannot consider either type in the same manner as beliefs, since they are unlikely to be threatened by discrepancies in one's experience. One can either play the piano or not, as Arthur Rubinstein reportedly said, and that's an end to it. You don't believe you can play the piano; you simply can. It is true that many skills may have required highly developed symbolizing activity for their acquisition, but they form part, not of a propositional structure of belief, but rather of a repertoire of action ability, (including, of course, mental activity). One's identity can certainly be attached in some degree to such skills, and, in the case of anyone who has devoted years to their acquisition, a very significant part. Undoubtedly, the continuity of meaning of any such skilled specialist can thus be profoundly threatened by illnesses, accidents, or other circumstances that prevent or curtail the exercising of a skill to which particular identity-significance is attached. The loss of a skill, or of the opportunity to exercise it, can have a powerful effect on one's feeling of personal effectiveness, and therefore on one's sense of continuous value.[7]

In taking stock of the different characteristics of skill, on the one hand, and primary frame belief on the other, however, we should not be distracted from the similar manner in which each set predisposes us to a particular kind of attention. Both skills and primary frame beliefs have determining effects on attitude. No surprise. All mental representations have implications for action.[8] This is simply another way of saying that what we believe about what we can perceive and what we can do both determines how we perceive the world, and how we act upon it. Skills are a special case, then, only insofar as they constitute also a dispositional *repertoire* for action.

In summary, it seems important to be aware that our insights into the dangers of specialized attention and activity would be less than valuable if they resulted on the one hand in what we might call a "pointing-the-finger" syndrome (that is, condemning what we cannot construe, simply because we cannot construe it), or on the other in a disqualification of any role for ourselves, *because* of our lack of a specific expertise. Specialized human disciplines are the outcome of a multiplicity of different human motives. Some of these are concerned with efforts to increase understanding, both of the physical world, and of ourselves. Others have necessarily emerged from efforts to increase the range and effectiveness of our perceptual and executive abilities. Yet others have arisen from efforts to give expression to elements in our human situation that elude other modes of investigation. All, of course, are expressive of particular interests. In all of these cases, the manner of selecting what is and is not important for our attention differs. Necessarily, different criteria apply. What is common, however, is that we may wrongly define what is relevant and what is not. Humankind is wrong about these classifications much more frequently than we would wish. Which of us has *not* erred through disregarding some aspect of a situation that turned out to be paramount? In short, it is not the simple existence of a skill that is subject to judgments as to its validity or its value. It is, rather, the matrix of belief within which the skill is used, together with the manner of its use, which is legitimately the object of such judgments.

Notwithstanding all these considerations, the process of learning—including learning from one's prior errors—depends not only upon the presence of feedback, but also upon our ability to register that feedback, to appraise it accurately, and to act upon that appraisal. Our earlier diagram (Figure One) did not purport to represent the feedback process; it portrayed the essential elements of human sensibility, rather than the dynamics of their interaction.

Up to this point, in fact, my emphasis has been upon *how* we come to represent to ourselves the actual state of the world in which we live (the world as fact), and the way it works (the world as process). As far as motives are concerned, I have simply concentrated on our desire to make sense. There are, however, two very different aspects to our sense-making: we first need to make sense in order to survive, but subsequently we make sense in order to fulfill ourselves in some way. Making sense is thus a necessary precondition for our being capable of pursuing any kind of "end." It is our determination of those ends that has, for the most part, determined what human beings have concentrated on doing for a large part of our species' history. Those ends, once basic survival needs have been satisfied, logically derive from the third class of propositions that each of us holds to be true: those that represent our beliefs about value.

In short, value has a powerful effect on what each of us experiences as essential to our sense of continuous meaningful identity. To an observer, then, anyone's continuity of belief is made apparent, not simply by evidence of our investment in protecting it, but also by the manner of our expressing it in positive action. Who we conceive ourselves to be is primarily revealed in what we actively *choose to do*. It is also revealed in our consciously choosing what we will *not* do. Those choices are evidenced in two ways: by an overall general commitment, and by the subsidiary activities that such a commitment requires; by, in effect, an overarching prescriptive "strategy," and by a range of subsidiary "tactics," whose exercise may require the acquisition and development of particular specialized modes of attention and focused skill. In sum, the exercising of any specific skill itself necessarily results from the nature of one's underlying commitment to a particular value-belief, and it is to the value-belief, rather than to the skill itself, that major elements of one's identity-continuity may be attached.

Thus far, it is probably amply apparent that my analysis has been determinedly neutral, and—as far as I can make it— objective. Here and there, inevitably, I will have revealed elements of my own primary frame beliefs, and my own interests. Consciously, I have tried to see these in the larger context, and consequently I have held back from asserting anything that could lead the reader to attribute to me any belief that could be interpreted only as self-serving. My own beliefs *are* of course self-serving, but I have been trying to indicate that such beliefs need not exclude motives that are respectful of other perspectives. It would be a shortcoming of virtually any program for improvement of the human condition if that program were to attribute problems to particular *groups* and to their centric motives rather than to the working of *processes* that are common to us all. Once again, we are brought up against the enormous importance of whether our engagement with one another is marked by *dissociative* or *associative* assumptions. It's an issue whose importance will continue to demand our attention.

In speaking of our ability to register feedback, to appraise it, and to act upon it, I am obviously using as my reference our three interdependent ambients. How can we characterize the influence of these three different domains in preventing particular kinds of feedback from modifying our approach to the world?

The unifying principles of self-protection in the three domains can be summarized succinctly:

– There are protective measures to prevent or curtail one's ability to *register* incongruity.

– There are protective measures to prevent or curtail one's ability to arrive at a valid *appraisal* of incongruity.

- There are protective maneuvers that promote one's ability to suppress *awareness* of incongruity, or distract from its importance.[9]

It is perhaps redundant to add that one cannot appraise something that one's senses have not registered, nor act to suppress an incongruity unless it has already been appraised as dangerous, albeit at a level that is below the threshold of our conscious awareness.

Let's look more closely at how these principles apply, restricting our concerns for the moment to the protection of *individual* continuities of meaning, but bearing in mind that these principles are relevant also to the ways in which a group continuity of meaning may be protected.

In the perceptual ambient, the possibilities seem to be as follows:

- One simply does not see, hear, smell, feel, or taste what is there to be seen, heard, smelled, felt, or tasted. Thus, "I didn't see him blush," "I didn't hear her," "I can't smell anything," "There isn't any breeze," "I can't taste anything." These may seem trivial examples, but each could be in partial defense of a belief. Our earlier example of the suppressing of awareness of particular words also belongs here.

- One may "manufacture" a sense percept: that is, one sees, hears, tastes, smells, or otherwise registers something that is not there. One's expectations for a particular outcome may result in our registering that outcome, even if it has not occurred. In his *The Vanishing Face of Gaia,* James Lovelock describes a remarkable example, in which both he and his wife experienced "seeing" a caravan on a beach close to their home in England, when there was in fact no caravan. Lovelock and his wife had been knowingly fearful of possible incursions by others into one of their own favorite places.

- One may distort a perception: that is, one may change its character, for example, by mishearing a sentence whose meaning is unacceptable.

In all of these cases, the protagonist is unaware of the error: that is, there is no *conscious* decision to deny or distort what is actually the case.

With reference to the ambient constituted of our concepts, and the manner in which they foster propositions about what we have experienced, the following are possible:

- We may *disregard* available sense evidence (by classifying it as irrelevant).

- We may *distort* the specific meaning of sense evidence in order to interpret it according to our preference: "He's not smiling. It's a sneer."

- We may *restrict* our ability to imagine new possibilities: that is, we can inhibit the imaginative and associative processes whereby new conceptualizations or new ways of combining ideas can be achieved: "I understand that perfectly well already."

- We may accord the feelings, perceptions, or beliefs of others more validity than our own, and thus *substitute* them for our own: "Two thousand observers *can't* be wrong."

- We may *project* aspects of our own feelings, attitudes, perceptions or beliefs onto others (that is, attribute to others what does not belong to them), and thus *disown* our personal experience. This will frequently take the form of attributing to others the cause of one's own discomfort, uneasiness, and misfortune ("No one's ever complained before!"), but neither is it rare for wishful thinking to result in *wrongly* attributing to others attitudes of sympathy, support, or encouragement.

In the action ambient, the possibilities are even more extensive.

– We can actively suppress or curtail our ability to act; for example, by *refusing* to look, listen, taste, touch, or smell; or to attend to particular bodily reactions, by conscious decision. (The inquisitorial panel deliberating upon whether or not Galileo was guilty of heresy refused to look through his telescope. Stephen Hawking was warned by the Pope that he should not further investigate the big bang hypothesis, since science has no business unveiling the mystery of God.[10])

– We can *withdraw* completely from the situation that is felt to be threatening. Agoraphobia is an obvious example.

– We can *distract* ourselves or others through activity that is irrelevant to the stressful situation: "Let's have a nice cup of tea." (Having a nice cup of tea is not always irrelevant, of course!)

– We can make *protective agreements* with others, for example, by inviting alliances that reciprocally reassure the allies that their beliefs are sound: "He's really got it in for us, hasn't he?"

– We can engage in *protective collusions* with others. I use the word "collusion" only in the sense of an agreement that is out-of-awareness. Collusions may be characterized as being either symmetrical or complementary in character, or having elements of both.

A *symmetrical* collusion is one in which the activity of (for example) each of two opposing participants is a mirror image of the activity of the other. Each metaphorically points a finger at the other as the source of a difficulty between them. Both in fact deny any responsibility for difficulties, in effect disowning an aspect of themselves. In due course, the very opposition of the other may thus itself come to be seen not only as further evidence for the correctness of one's own view, but also as justification for the use of extreme measures to redress the presumed offense. It's probable that most of us, at some point in our own lives, will have experienced at least one episode of such a sort, most likely in childhood. In adulthood, it is a not uncommon phenomenon in dysfunctional marriages.

Complementary collusions are those in which the participants take complementary roles in relation to one another. One projects, the other introjects. All of the negative factors are attributed to one of the participants; all of the positive factors to the other. Both collude in this distribution of responsibilities, the one by denying any negatives in their own behavior, the other by disowning any positives in theirs. Neither has any motive to modify this allocation of blame and blamelessness, since the continuity of meaning of each is affirmed. One sees him or herself as a blameless person. The other sees him or herself as perpetually responsible for the dissatisfaction of the other. Do Laurel and Hardy come to mind?[11]

Both sorts of collusion may be stable in character, or unstable. Collusions that involve two participants or parties tend to be more stable than those involving three or more participants or parties, as these latter forms often involve shiftings of roles between the participants, or changes in who is involved in the collusive network. The prototype of such networks has been powerfully described and analyzed by Claude Steiner as a victimizer/victim/rescuer triad.[12] To be designated a victimizer or a rescuer presumes a victim. To be a victim presumes a victimizer. The roles shift somewhat when a victim unknowingly refuses to be rescued, and thus victimizes the potential rescuer. The rescuer may then move on to a more accessible victim, thus freeing up the network to incorporate another aspiring rescuer. Other variants may involve bevies of rescuers, and other varieties of protective maneuverings for each of the participants. Many of us are, in fact, ambivalent enough about ourselves that we will reverberate between opposing identity-modes. The rescuer may become a victim; the victim a victimizer. All three may also consciously try to forge protective alliances with others. Each may at different times introject or project different aspects of one another.

Realistically, in everyday life, "pure" cases of such alignments are probably rarer than more confused cases. Ambivalence and uncertainty mark the edges of primary frame assumptions about identity, and ambivalence is characteristically manifested by reverberation between the alternative identity-beliefs. In such cases, collusions, alliances, projections, and introjections may seem to meet, disperse, reform, and alternate in a complex dance of relationship interactions, depending as much on happenstance as on choice.

In describing such complex protective behaviors, we may tend to forget that any potential collusive relationship, or network of relationships, by definition requires the consent of a partner or partners, each of whom is protecting a particular view of reality, and involving other people in that protectionism. It follows, then, that not being seduced by an invitation to collude, or rejecting a protective alliance, are acts that promote the possibility of change. They are negations that assert the commitment to *ownership*, to a recognizing of one's own responsibility for self. They are positive assertions of the need for honesty in relationships with one another. Unfortunately, many of our social conventions put these commitments at risk. Undoubtedly modern society itself participates in extensive collusive structures that protect established belief.[13]

Avoiding participation in the processes encouraged by these structures is necessary if we are to become free of the virtual realities they foster. We would be foolish, though, to underestimate the difficulties of committing ourselves to such a course, since the participants in collusions—possibly including we ourselves— might have a strong identity investment in preserving them.

There is a special kind of irony, I suppose, in registering that the very symbolizing ability that characterizes human sensibility is itself the source of our ability to disown our actual realities, and substitute virtual worlds for them. If we react to others by professing to be other than what we are, we place barriers in the way of truly meeting one another, and therefore one another's unique perspective on reality. It is true that we do engage in such dishonest behavior with one another because of our individual assessments of the costs of behaving (in effect, of *being*) otherwise. If we behave deceptively, it is because the costs of behaving in such a manner are acceptable to us; the continuity of a particular meaning for our own individual identity is subjectively felt to be more important.[14]

All human behavior, of course, regardless of whether consciously or unconsciously motivated, results from a balancing of risks against advantage. Figure Two illustrates how different kinds of assignment or acceptance of responsibility result in different kinds of cost.

Part of my reason for representing these attitudinal choices graphically, and without regard to their specific circumstances, is that I want to avoid the too-easy quick moral condemnation of the particular kinds of choices people make. Without knowing the full reality of another's experience of life, how can we possibly claim to judge whether that person has made the best decisions possible? We must always remind ourselves that the kind of sense anyone makes, *makes sense to them*. Each of us may be presumed to have been willing to pay such costs as we are aware of. In sum, then:

- It is only when we assess the costs to ourselves and find that we underestimated them that we may be motivated to change;

VICISSITUDES IN THE RECOGNITION OF RESPONSIBILITY

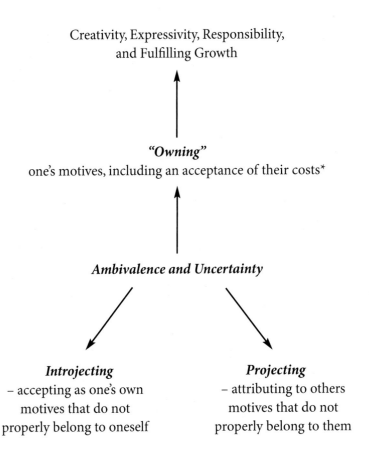

Creativity, Expressivity, Responsibility,
and Fulfilling Growth

"Owning"
one's motives, including an acceptance of their costs*

Ambivalence and Uncertainty

Introjecting
– accepting as one's own
motives that do not
properly belong to oneself

Projecting
– attributing to others
motives that do not
properly belong to them

The arrows indicate the directions of possible choice.
* "Costs" can only be recognized accurately when responsibility is
assigned correctly.

- It is only when the costs of a particular person's or group's behavior are paid by others that society itself starts to take an interest;

- It is only when the costs of a particular person's or group's behavior are paid by the rest of humanity that humankind itself begins to pay attention.

In defense of a particular continuity of identity, then, it must be borne in mind that suppressing awareness of incongruity is driven by the need to deny any awareness of costs. Whether that denial involves the costs to oneself, to others, or to both self and other, will depend on the nature of the belief that is being protected.

In the case of behavior that serves selfish interests, a protagonist person or group will naturally be concerned with hiding the costs of those interests from others, since costs paid by others are of no concern to them. Obviously, the simplest way to prevent interested parties from being aware of costs is to deprive them of information, or actively misinform them, just as we do with ourselves when it is we who are fearful of change.

I hope it will be apparent, even as we consider this daunting list of ways in which given primary frame beliefs can be preserved, that there is a potentially reassuring similarity of pattern. The pattern is easily obscured by the individual complexities of protective maneuverings, because we are of course distracted by our concerns about the immediate circumstances, and thus in many cases will be unable to sustain an off-centered perspective. Centrically motivated activity *by definition* excludes other considerations.

What is the critical common feature evident in every kind of identity-protecting maneuver? It seems that the common feature is determined by the very discriminating criterion of identity itself, which consists primarily of where we draw the line of distinction between what we experience as "self" and what we experience as "other." For human beings, that line does not simply coincide with one's physical boundary. It also follows the contours of our emotional and symbolic connection to others. When we protect our continuity of identity, then, we are also protecting our conceptualization of where the boundary of that identity lies. Since one's sense of identity is not only arrived at through experiencing an unchanging element in one's self over time, but also through a complex sense of the nature of our affiliations, fellowships, and kinship with, or alienation from others, we need to take into account the manner in which affiliations and disaffiliations can affect where we set the boundary limits of our identities. In some cases, we may even come to consider that it is a particular affiliation with another, or others, rather than some independent characteristic in ourselves, that defines who we are. In other cases, we may define ourselves rather on the basis of our very *alienation* from others.

The identity of any one of us is thus expressive of the nature of the balance of independence, interdependence, and dependence characteristic of our relationship with others. Whether we experience that balance as having been determined primarily by ourselves or primarily by others, is obviously likely to be a major factor in our openness or resistance to the possibility of change.

Let's examine in closer detail the manner in which the dynamics of our affiliations with others affects that balance, and thus whether we will be able to free ourselves from mistaken formulations of reality, or cling tenaciously to the sense we've already made.

8

Cooperation

THE SUPREME ACHIEVEMENT of human symbolic processes, declared Langer, is cooperation. The word itself, of course, means "working together." Working together may nevertheless have very different connotations for those living in different social, professional, and political circumstances. Cooperation in a democracy will differ radically from cooperation within a dictatorship. The term may also have very different connotations for those working together within a given social, professional, or political organization. Many different kinds of cooperative endeavor are possible, both between organizations and within them, and some of those kinds are certainly not egalitarian.

Although the idea of cooperation primarily calls to mind agreement about a common purpose, it is important to remember that particular common purposes may be neither to an individual's interest nor to that of the cooperating group. Common purposes may, for example, consist of efforts to defend shared fundamental identity-beliefs. Just as an individual can mobilize every personal resource to protect a continuity of identity, so too can any group similarly organize to protect itself from the critical feedback it receives from beyond its self-defined boundary. And, just as with individuals, a group's purpose may reflect in some respects its commitment to more satisfying realizations of human potential, and in others its protectiveness of a continuous set of primary frame beliefs that are inimical to such realizations.

In both cases, however, our understanding of the forces affecting our ability to cooperate with one another, or to oppose one another, can be furthered by considering the types of affiliative relational form that determine what kinds of cooperation can occur. Those forms will also have implications for the stability or instability of the kinds of cooperation they promote.

It is possible, I think, to distinguish five major types of communal affiliation.

The first of these is *fortuitous affiliation*, where the time and geographic location of one's birth, and the accidental determination of one's gender, social situation, ethnic group, nationality, and so on, place us in a context that was not of our own choosing. These are all powerful factors in the establishment of identity, and at some point in our lives, most of us will be made acutely conscious of them.

I am aware, of course, that there are belief systems in which some of these statements will be considered incorrect. For any readers who hold to such beliefs, it may be helpful to understand that I am simply attempting to summarize what constitutes the *untutored* experience each of us has *subjectively* of our own reality.

Whatever one's personal stance in relation to the significance of such reservations, however, there are clearly three fundamental fortuitous affiliations that, although shared by all of us, we are often prone to banish from our everyday consciousness. This habitual disregard has cost humanity dearly, and continues do so, since it has contributed to our sustaining of centric preoccupations beyond their serviceability to humankind. Our ignorance can best be described by summarizing its consequences: we have been able to act as if we were a law only unto ourselves. That we have been able to do so can be attributed directly to our neglect of those fundamental affiliations, namely:

– Our affiliation with one another as human beings.

– Our affiliation with all other forms of life: that is, with life itself.

– Our affiliation with the universe, with all that is.

We'll return to considering the wider implications of these neglected affiliations in our final chapter. Their major importance is that they cannot be used to promote polarizations between different loyalties. That is, they are representative of a higher order of cooperation than the kinds that derive from purely protective motives.

The second kind of affiliation is one that is *knowingly chosen*, as when we get together with like-minded others to achieve purposes expressive of our interests, and which are seen to require more for their realization than the efforts and activity of a single person. Such affiliations both express and affirm the identity of all the participants. All involved share a common objective, and all are (other things being equal) freely committed to its realization. Even here, however, we need to remember that the continuity of belief being affirmed may not be without serious error. On the one hand, knowingly chosen affiliations can contribute (indeed, have contributed) to the vast expansions of the human ambient brought about by systematic scientific, philosophical, and artistic activity; on the other, many can—and have—contributed to restrictions of potential enquiry and curtailments of human freedom. Indeed, some chosen affiliations can *promote* the dissociation from others that characterizes human conflict.

The third kind of affiliation is that which is *unknowingly chosen*. The collusive interactions in which we may engage in order to sustain faulty beliefs are a prime example. There is also, however, a more positive variety of unknowing pattern in relationships. We are able to create positive patterns of interaction with little or no awareness, as when our fundamental assumptions about value, and perhaps interest, foster the right kinds of circumstances for expressive, creative, constructive, or even playful cooperative activity to occur. These types of relationships, and the benefits that ensue, occur primarily when the participants are functioning un-defensively, and thus are either open-minded about the possibilities inherent in a given situation, or are actively pursuing a course of action that expresses and fulfills their positive engagement with the world. The least obvious of such relationships are probably those in which the participants share fundamental beliefs about *process*, and therefore slip easily into cooperative activity that is guided by those beliefs, rather than the more obvious occasions when cooperative activity is guided by the conscious sharing of particular values or particular interests. In that sense, all engaged in reading this book could be considered to be affiliated with each other, simply because of their common willingness to take its ideas seriously and their preparedness to question fundamental assumptions about themselves. In sum, unconscious affiliations are not necessarily indicative of protective motives, and many are to be celebrated.

The fourth kind is *unwilling affiliation*. It is produced by *coercion*, as when threat of force, force itself, or some other kind of curtailment of individual liberty is used by any agent, but most particularly a society, an institution, or an oligarchy, to achieve acquiescence or compliance to further or protect its own interests. Such enforced affiliations depend on the denial of individual freedom. The cooperation they produce can most appropriately be thought of as a kind of psychic enslavement, endured only because no viable course of alternative action seems possible.

The fifth kind is that of *contracted affiliation*. In this type, an individual is willing to participate in serving the objectives of some larger group in exchange for some acceptable token of value. One agrees to forego, defer, or modify the satisfaction of some personal objective or objectives in exchange for some universally-tradable token (like money) or a more intangible token (like fame, public recognition, favored treatment of some kind, power, or reciprocal services). Services can be traded, of course, without any affiliative significance being assigned to them. The participants simply recognize that each is engaging in a relationship based on a willingness to cooperate in order to achieve a deferred personal objective. The participants do not cooperate to achieve a common purpose, but to achieve different purposes, and their relationship carries no other meaning than their common recognition that each can be useful to the other, at least for the duration of a single transaction. Longer-lasting contractual agreements can, however, be considered affiliative, because they promote the experience of a particular kind of continuity of meaning and thus undoubtedly have a greater significance for identity. The most common manifestation of such contracted affiliation in modern society is probably one's job.

As in our earlier discrimination of discrete categories, we must be careful not to conclude that all forms of affiliation or cooperation can be easily or accurately allocated to a particular box. Many of our affiliations will have the characteristics of more than one type, and over time, affiliations that began in one mode can be transformed. An affiliation that began as a freely chosen one can begin to take on a contractual character, or even a coercive one.[1] A fortuitous affiliation may well entrain contractual obligations, some of which will be experienced as freely chosen. An unknowing affiliation can become conscious, a conscious one decline into familiar habit. It is important to register, too, that an affiliation may be experienced as being of one kind, when it is in fact of another kind. Affiliations may result from our being actively deceived as to their true nature.

All affiliations, of course, have implications for the identities of the people who constitute them. The most powerful factor in influencing the nature of those identities is probably whether an affiliation affirms an individual's sense of personal effectiveness, or negates it. Clearly, in this regard, the different affiliative forms may have very different implications. Fortuitous affiliations will have a very different character from ones that are knowingly chosen. Unwilling affiliations can hardly enhance or affirm a sense of effectiveness for any other than the coercive agents themselves. Notwithstanding these variants, I think we may also assert that in all affiliative forms the individual characters of those who together constitute an identifiable group entity also affect the nature of that identity. How these individual persons in their interactions affect the willingness or unwillingness of the group itself to change will depend, not only on what kind of functional purpose an individual serves for the group, but also what kind of purpose the affiliative entity serves for each individual within it. Just as our membership in a nation, an organized religion, an alumni association, or a soccer team affects what we are willing to expect of ourselves and of others, so, too, does our membership in humankind.

The clearest examples of organization expressing human cooperative endeavor are those that have been consciously organized ("instituted") to achieve a particular purpose. They may be thought of as planned social "mechanisms" for the efficient achievement of a shared goal. We probably call such organizations institutions because they fixedly designate, limit, prescribe, and thus bureaucratize the human actions and interactions which are seen to be the most efficient way of achieving the agreed-upon common objectives.

It is the purpose or purposes for which an organization exists, then, that can be said to constitute the matrix within which are set its primary frame beliefs about fact, process, and value. Specifically, then, what tends to be bureaucratized in any institution will not only be the values that led to its formation in the first place, but the process beliefs that define how its purposes might be most efficiently achieved, including beliefs about the nature of cooperation itself. Consequently, just as an individual may be unable to sustain an off-centered perspective when in the middle of a demanding action-mode, so may an institution, whose fundamental assumptions about how to get something done are enshrined in its structure, tend to resist an observing awareness of its processes. In short, functional efficiency may be achieved only at the cost of awareness of overall context.

Necessarily, the process of bureaucratization always involves a selective suppression of feedback, in order to prevent the functioning units of the cooperating group from being distracted from concentrating on their specific tasks. Since the goal is efficiency of executive function in relation to an already-established objective, conceptual, perceptual, and executive functions that are considered irrelevant to the task at hand are severely circumscribed. These restrictions take on a variety of forms in human organizations, but it is possible to map some universals: the restriction of individual human activity to specialized functional roles; the automatizing of repetitive tasks; the removal of "irrelevant" feedback between functional units; and the assessment of outcomes according to predetermined criteria. All are characteristic.[2]

In effect, then, such bureaucratizing procedures may *institutionalize* the disregarding of inconvenient feedback, and possibly, even, its suppression. Bureaucratization may be thought of as "legislating" the containment of pockets of activity, sustaining the fiction that these affect only those aspects of their surroundings that are deemed to be relevant to the task at hand. Other aspects are treated as if they do not exist. As in Nature, however, the exclusion of some aspect of reality from an entity's ambient does not mean that it is irrelevant. Negated aspects of the environment may be removed from consideration, but they cannot be obliterated. The environment has a way of asserting its presence without regard to the convenience of subjective purpose, or vested interest.

Conceptually, shifting our focus from individual identity to organizational identity requires only a small adjustment, since we can use the same conceptual scheme for analyzing institutions as we previously used for better understanding the ways in which individual people make sense. We can, in fact, map the dynamics of the factors involved in the creation of institutional identity by looking in a slightly different manner at Figure One.

In Figure One (page 30), we were looking at the factors that interact to produce a more-or-less coherent internal representation of what we hold to be true about the world. That representation, summarily characterized in the center of the figure, we spoke of as constituting the framework within which an individual person would make his or her own particular kind of sense. If, then, every particular detail of an individual's experience and capabilities were mapped out upon the diagram, and the space in the center occupied by an inventory of all the propositions making up that person's beliefs, we could say that we had—at least at one particular moment—a summary representation of that person's identity. Although in the real world any such summary would be impossible to achieve, most of us in our desire to understand others almost routinely attempt something along those lines, just as in this book I attempt something similar in relation to humankind itself.

To analyze an institutional structure, we may take the same diagram, and, replacing the term "individual" with the term "institution," use it to summarize that institution's internal representation of the world. The center of the diagram would thus now comprise an inventory of the propositional beliefs summarizing the identity of the institution. As with an individual, then, it is those beliefs that will determine what an organization pays attention to, how it thinks, and what it does. However, there is of course a major difference from the earlier diagram. For an institution, the functioning of each of its ambients, conceptual, perceptual, and executive, depends on the *people* who have been assigned those particular functions, or who have assumed them. Figure Three summarizes these differences.

THE CONSTITUENTS OF AN INSTITUTION'S WORLD

Perceptual Ambient
(The world that can be registered by those
who have accepted circumscribed
perceptual functions that accord with the
institution's definition of purpose)

↓

The institution's total internal
representation of itself
and the world permitted by
the interaction of all three ambients

Conceptual Ambient
(The world of concepts
permitted by the
founding definition
of institutional purpose)

Action Ambient
(The world of action
permitted by the
founding definition
of institutional purposes)

The overall procedural assumption of any human institution is that cooperation enables us to achieve together what it would be more difficult and perhaps impossible for any single one of us to achieve alone. This assumption follows inevitably from the realization that our symbolizing abilities, which have extraordinary power to enhance and facilitate human communication, enable us to inform, educate, and persuade one another, as well as cajole, order, or inflame. We can then, in effect, multiply our executive abilities beyond the relatively puny power of the individual. Many observers working systematically together can perceive more than a single individual, many thinkers can facilitate conceptual exploration, and many actors can extend the range and power of our effectiveness.

These increments of human ability effectively enlarge every element of the human ambient. They can, however, only be brought about when, however amorphously, different individuals can agree upon a common purpose, or knowingly share common interests. Indeed, the shared discovery of complex similar or identical purposes itself depends on symbolic communication.

There are clear structural consequences for both the formal and informal cooperations that can result from agreeing upon a common purpose. We've already identified the bureaucratic implications, but to these we should also add two that pertain more to the individual members of a cooperating group, namely, that:

– Other individual purposes may temporarily need to be set aside in order to achieve effective cooperation.

– Antagonistic individual purposes will also need to be set aside.

To summarize: since for any organization the conceptualizations affecting common purpose are a feature of its very inception, the anticipated conceptual, perceptual, and action functions of the organization are formally restricted to those that directly bear on the carrying out of that previously established purpose. Thus, although every individual person of course has his or her own perceptual, conceptual, and action abilities, only some of these will be considered relevant to the cooperative purpose. From the institution's point of view, it is the role that individuals carry in relation to institutional purpose that defines them, not who they actually are as whole human beings. There is thus almost inevitably a potential dehumanizing element to any institution's manner of defining its constituent members.

Treating of institutions as perceiving, thinking, and acting systems can greatly simplify our understanding of the way they function. However, there are still some dangers; in particular, we may consider the identity of an institution to be directly analogous to the identity of an individual.

In the case of both institutions and individuals, of course, it is also important to realize that identity can be assigned on the basis of two entirely different perspectives on one's being-in-the-world: one's identity as experienced from within; and one's identity as perceived from without. Seen from outside, an identity may be clearly seen in relation to its context, but it may also alternatively be seen in the light of the beliefs of the observer, and therefore have attributed to it characteristics which it does not in fact have. Indeed, both the possessor of an identity and an external observer of that identity can be wrong about its true nature. In the case of an institution, there is of course no single observing consciousness, but many; so, even internally, there may be different perceptions of what that identity really is. When considering institutions and other similar organizational forms, then, we must be careful to remember that, even though an institution may have a particular publicly perceived identity, that identity may be quite different from the one individual members of the institution attribute to it.

Notwithstanding these different perspectives, there is a crucial fundamental difference between individuals and institutions.

Both may be analyzed similarly as different forms of perceptual, thinking, and action systems, but their similarity of experiential form does not coincide with what we may perhaps characterize as their existential quality. To attribute to each the same kind of existential quality is a grave error. The ramifications of that error, and the failure to recognize it, are far-reaching, for it is an error that can lead to faulty beliefs on the part of members of institutions about both how they should relate to their other component members and how they should relate to the institution. The best summary of the crucial difference between individuals and the cooperative institutional structures we form is evidently easily forgotten, but nevertheless stunningly obvious:

An institution does not exist as a life form, a being, and therefore does not feel, does not suffer, cannot fall ill, or die, or experience pain or joy. We often speak of institutions as if they can, and unfortunately thus lose sight of the reality that it is we, the human beings who constitute them, who may intensely feel, on our own behalf, fulfillment, frustration, pain, and so on, **in the degree to which our own identities are involved.**

The crucial fact is that an organization, unlike an individual, does not have an existential identity, but only an abstract one. This is why a significant part of the activity of particular members of an organization may be allocated to devising and promulgating the use of quite arbitrary or accidental *symbols* of the group's identity in order to create the illusion of a physical presence: flags; ceremonies; distinctive dress; logos; labels; titles; stereotyped awards. The purpose of such activity is to promote loyalty to the group identity, and thus to the particular set of beliefs about value, fact, and process that are consistent with the organization's purpose. The loyalty of a group's members is a powerful factor in contributing to its ability to resist disconfirming feedback from the environment. Indeed, if individual members of an institution associate their senses of self with their affiliation to the institution, hostile environmental response can be a major factor in ensuring institutional solidarity.

Endowing any institution with the metaphorical attributes of a human being may, ironically, remind us also of a mirror-image error we've already identified, and one with which most of us are already only too familiar: the belief that the individual people who make up the institution may be considered not as people, but simply as mechanisms for carrying out institutional functions. This is perhaps illustrative of an even greater irony: it is owing to the character of the process of symbolic representation itself that humans can not only anthropomorphize their institutions, but also, attending solely to institutional purposes, dehumanize one another.

In this regard, it is important to consider the ramifications of what was discerned at the end of the last chapter. The threat to an organization's continuity of belief is structurally similar to a threat to individual identity, and many of the ways in which threatening feedback can be set aside are also similar. The most significant threat to institutional identity, however, is a threat to its purpose, its very reason for being. The equivalent threat for an individual human being would be being treated by others as if one had no justification for being alive. As with a human infant, disaffirmed in such a way by a parent or a caregiver, it is difficult to think how an organization could survive a massive disaffirmation of its purpose for existing at all.

The primary frame beliefs of an institution (treated, still, as a discrete identifiable entity) will also include its assumptions about what is necessary to promote efficiency in the execution of predetermined tasks. (These, to reiterate, are the curtailing of attention towards apparent irrelevancies, and the concentrating of focus on the job at hand.) I hope it will already be obvious that these assumptions would also be vulnerable to untidy feedback from a recalcitrant world.

It may well be that an efficient organization will have special-ized functional structures in place to deal with a certain amount of (predicted) recalcitrance. Tom Wolfe wrote an entertaining essay on the phenomenon, called "Mau-Mauing the Flak-Catchers"; the title best translates, I think, to something like "Terrorizing the Public-Relations Personnel." Wolfe was suggesting that many organizations have designated employees whose primary function is to avert, discredit, or otherwise render harmless the critical flak likely to be thrown at it by other parts of society. He also suggested that, if the recalcitrance were unpredictable, or vastly larger than anticipated, the flak-catchers would be overwhelmed, and the organization would consequently have to scramble for ways to deal with the threat. In such a circumstance, Wolfe postulated that the flak-catchers, as a necessary part of an institution's defenses, would also, necessarily, be expendable. In other words, an institution could cushion itself from the effects of threatening feedback by condemning the flak-catchers as incompetent (and firing them if necessary), thus gaining time by requiring those who were dissatisfied with the institution's behavior to begin their process of criticism anew. (Does the sacrificial tail of the lizard spring to mind?)

An institution's repertoire of protective procedures may also be brought into play to deal with discrepant experience within its constituent parts. Feedback between the constituent parts of an organization, which is analogous to the feedback between the parts of an organism, may, in the case of perceived threats to the integrity of the organizing entity, result, just as with similar threats from the environment, in protective maneuvers ranging from the mild to the severe. An institution's available ploys may be many, and in many cases they can be seen to resemble those available to an individual.

There are also, however, ploys of a different order. An institu-tion can, for example, appoint a committee, withdraw necessary funding or facilities from a discomforting person or group, modify job descriptions, and promote, demote, or reassign a person with critical abilities. *In extremis,* such persons may be "retired," "fired," "let go," or "terminated." This last term, we have now come to realize, can be a euphemism for something much darker. All such maneuvers are made possible by the institution's ability to control the form of its separate functional divisions, the information made available to them, and the manner in which those divisions are permitted to operate in relation to one another.

For an organization, however, protective maneuvers in relation to its constituent parts have different consequences than they would have for an organism, which is of course limited in the number of body parts or systems towards which it can behave so trenchantly. We do not pluck out our eyes if they offend us. (We can, however, direct them to look elsewhere.) An organization, however, can, at least in theory and if the circumstances are right, replace its parts (i.e., its people) almost indefinitely, since it is safeguarding only functions. This is much like an axe, which continues to function as an axe, even though its head and its shaft have been frequently replaced. Again we must remind ourselves, however, that it is not the institution that behaves in this way; it is particular individuals or sub-groups of people who determine such actions, based on their view of what will best benefit the corporate group (and thus themselves). When we defend our institutions, our organizations, our nations, and our cultures against potentially corrective feedback, we do so only insofar as our own continuity of personal meaning is felt to be under attack.

The human consequences of an institution's defensive maneuvers can be devastating, not only for the individuals concerned, but also for the society in which the institution functions. The dynamic always involves a suppression of any off-centered observing awareness. In this regard, an organization is quite different from an organism, for the subsidiary systems of an organism have no awareness themselves of the whole creature of which they are parts. The subsidiary parts of an organization, since they are made up of people, are by contrast always at least potentially able to consider their own contextual relationship with their colleagues, and their participation in the institution's relationship with its environment. That is, they *are* capable of appraising their own functions in relation to the whole.

The self-awareness of a human being necessarily resides in that person's consciousness, the coordinating awareness of the whole person. However, individual consciousness is primarily appraising and causal; that is, concerned with the organism's management of its own purposes in relation to its ambient, which includes the motives and actions of other creatures. In the case of an institution, managing its purposes in relation to its environment will tend to be seen rather as the specialized task of a specific sub-group or groups than of the organization as a whole. Causal awareness will not be a designated function of any others, even if those others are in some cases better placed to appraise the impact of the institution on its surrounding world. In short, there is no appraising or causal institutional self directly analogous to the self of an individual human being. Public relations personnel are more likely to be charged with promoting the organization's objectives in the outside world than with providing potentially disruptive feedback to a board of directors or other controlling group.

In effect, then, the individual causal awareness of the members of an institution will have an effect, desired or not, on their functional relationship with the whole. Similarly, by design or not, the institution has an impact upon its members, independent of their designated function. In organizations having an almost inexhaustible supply of spare parts (read "people"), such impacts might simply be disregarded by those in the organization's hierarchy with thinking functions in regard to policy and process, because sensitivity to such impacts would distract attention from the institution's efficient pursuit of its purpose. The effect of long hours, for example, or bad working conditions, toxic environments, and poor remuneration would be easy for the higher managers in a manufacturing company to disregard in periods of high unemployment, or in circumstances where employees might be particularly vulnerable to other forces in their life situations. One readily thinks of the examples of indentured labor, immigrant labor, and ethnic vulnerability to exploitation. All such conditions have been variously disregarded or exploited in the course of history, and are still being disregarded more pervasively than any of us should feel any equanimity about. Evidently, institutions can be as centrically preoccupied as any individual creature. In the institutional case, however, it will be a controlling group that acts centrically, and in such a way that individual hardship for other sub-parts is disregarded.[3]

Throughout large parts of the range of human cooperative endeavor, it is nevertheless apparent that due care can be given, and has been, to the wellbeing of those individual humans who effectively contribute to the institution's achievement of its purposes. Given the symbolic meanings attributed to human institutions, it is not surprising that such care is evidenced primarily by the provision of symbolic rewards and recognition for dedicated commitment and service. From the very smallest to the largest of human institutions, we give honors, rewards, prizes, and praise to those who impeccably carry out institutional functions. In contrast, symbolic rewards have no relevance at all to the effective functioning of any human individual's own sub-systems, although I confess I have on occasion murmured approval to my lungs or muscles after a strenuous activity of some kind. I don't think this produces any effect, since my muscles and lungs, after all, have no way of registering such symbolic approval. My care for my subsidiary systems depends more on my feeding or exercising them sufficiently than on singing their praises.

It is also true for institutional systems, however, that their subsidiaries will work better with the right kind of "food" or "exercise," that is, with direct physical benefits of some kind, or, at least no real neglect of what is needed for a sense of wellbeing. In human societies, symbolic rewards may be pervasively used to enhance loyalty, but there will be times when the neglect of the more physical factors has its comeuppance. Even nurses will on occasion strike for more money. Since it is, of course, particularly difficult for people in service professions to admit to any self-serving motive, the rhetoric associated with strike action in such cases tends to emphasize the effects of poor pay on the quality of service, rather than on the standard of living of the profession's members. However, it is a characteristic of such professionals that they, almost uniquely, will strike or demonstrate, not for greater benefits for themselves, but for the sake of the quality of service they are committed to providing.

It emerges then, and not surprisingly, that all individuals may have a kind of hierarchy within which their various affiliations are organized. In the case of nurses and other care professionals, greater identity significance may be attached to the values expressed in their profession than to the contracted affiliations they necessarily become involved with in order to make a living.

Any of us may in fact find ourselves in situations where our fundamental values and perhaps interests are at odds with those of the organizations or institutions to which we are affiliated. In such cases, several different options may be available to us. We may, for example, dissociate ourselves from those aspects of the organization or institution that are offensive to us, and take personal refuge in the belief that we can have no responsibility in relation to those aspects because they do not impinge on our own functional role. We may similarly continue to function in the organization because of sanctions of some kind (whether real or threatened). Alternatively, we may attempt to change the organization, or sabotage its ability to act on values to which we do not subscribe. We may also, of course, simply attempt to discontinue our affiliation and follow our own purposes more consistently elsewhere.[4] All of these variations can apply in relation to any human association, from the intimately small to the very largest: from one's family, for example, to nations, cultures, and, indeed, humankind itself.

When it comes to the protection of one's continuity of meaning against threat, however, it must be acknowledged that institutions are vastly more powerful in their ability to resist dissonant feedback from individuals than individuals are to resist similar feedback from institutions. It is true that the recent history of humankind has seen advances in understanding the moral obligations each theoretically has to the other, but statements summarizing such understanding of responsibility are still pervasively disregarded by those of us whose centric concerns obliterate any larger awareness. We do now have a "universal" declaration of human rights, and the so-called Nuremberg Principles (which affirm the moral responsibility of the individual in global terms rather than local ones), but the lone individual who decries the purposes or procedures of an institution on the basis of its violation of some universal standard of moral conduct is nevertheless in today's world more likely to be victimized than attended to. Perhaps I should rather say "victimized locally and praised only elsewhere." Aung San Sun Kyi may have been awarded the Nobel Peace Prize, but she is at the time of this writing still under house arrest in her own country, and, as I review this very sentence, the military government of that country is brutally suppressing peaceful pro-democracy demonstrations in the streets.

I'm afraid that giving even a very few examples of institutional resistance to critical feedback from principled individuals makes for very depressing reading. Tough-minded readers may be referred to the book by Broad and Wade in the bibliography for examples. Others still may be able to sustain a reading of the enquiry report on the Westray mine disaster in Nova Scotia, Canada, in May 1992, in which twenty-six coal miners were killed as a result of an underground explosion. The executive summary of that report, "The Westray Story: A Predictable Path to Disaster," was at the time of this writing still available on the Internet. It is a moving inventory of the ways in which individuals and institutions can justify their failure to meet their responsibilities to one another.[5]

We'll return in our final chapter to a wider consideration of the significance of human affiliations, both for our individual identities, and for the destiny of our species, but at the moment there is a more immediate claim on our attention. Given all the vagaries of the elements that, interacting with one another, make up our ability to make sense, what can we deduce with some conviction about how to make better sense than we presently do? That is, not only to make better sense as personally experienced selves, but also as the entire human collective in relation to its position in the universe?

Thus far, and throughout, we have focused primarily on the manner in which continuities of belief, both individual and institutional, are formed and defended. We have yet to consider how they may be changed.

9

Change

"CHANGE" is a powerful word. It arouses strong feelings. It's scarcely possible to itemize these in their entirety, but it is possible to characterize them by where they sit on the range of possibilities. If we are afraid of change, we do not reach out for it, nor give it welcome. If we are hopeful of what change can bring, we both seek it, and embrace it when it is realized. It is fear and hope, then, that are the extremities of the range of emotions with which we may have to deal, both in regards to change for ourselves, and change elsewhere.

I am arguing, of course, that the critical difference between the two extremes can be related to whether change, as anticipated by any individual person or even groups of persons, is considered to be a threat to an already-established identity, and consequently to be feared, or is continuous with it, and thus affirms, endorses, or permits a deeper realization of it. The fear associated with change is always a fear of loss of meaningful continuity. Hope is its antithesis. It is the expectation of gain, a greater fulfillment. It is thus our relative weighting of these two factors that most accurately summarizes at any particular moment the nature of our motives.

Those motives are largely determined for all of us by what any kind of change is considered to be a change *from*. A change from something good to something bad is obviously very different from a change from something bad to something good. How we differentiate good and bad from one another, however, necessarily depends on what we already believe. It may be that it is our very definition of those concepts that is seriously at fault, and thus costly, both to ourselves and to others.

Although our task here is mostly to discern what is necessary in principle to foster a change *away* from something that has previously carried heavy costs, and thus *towards* a more positive engagement with the world, there are other occasions when our task may not be to discover a new way of being, but rather to *recover* from the disruption of a continuity that has been lost. In both kinds of situations, however, the most fundamental of the forces affecting our motives is our need to experience ourselves as having some ability to influence the course of events in our lives; in other words, to be *effective*, to make a difference, to be in charge of our lives, rather than being victims of circumstances and events that are beyond our control.

The urge to feel effective thus has two important implications for us, roughly depending on which of the above situations we are likely to find ourselves in. The first is that sometimes a major change in fundamental belief is only likely to occur after a period of more-or-less protracted dissatisfaction, uneasiness, or uncertainty. (We illustrated this in Figure Two [page 107] by placing the pivotal position of uncertainty in the center of the diagram.) However, when we feel uncertain, we feel ineffective; that is why it is difficult for us to sustain uncertainty for very long. It's no surprise, then, that in situations where our uneasiness is hard to sustain, the urgent desire for a quick solution, a quick resolution, may itself persuade us to jump into action before the assumptions implicit in our action can be adequately considered. To get something done, regardless of its effectiveness—or even, on occasion, its relevance—is always, however tenuously, an affirmation of one's self. As we noted earlier, we may on occasion be particularly vulnerable to exhortations from others offering us the promise of such effectiveness.

The second implication is in regard to those situations where we have experienced a sudden and devastating loss: one that brings home to us our ultimate helplessness in the face of cataclysmic circumstance. The death or serious illness of a significantly important person may be the precipitating cause, but anything that contributes to our feeling that we have lost or could easily lose something essential to our overall wellbeing can make us feel that the solid ground underneath our feet has shifted irrevocably, and we can't regain our footing. It is not only the loss of a dear partner or child that may affect us so profoundly. The loss of a significant skill to which our identity is attached, the loss of an important job, the loss of physical or mental functioning by reason of an accident or illness—any of these, or any similarly devastating discontinuity, has the potential to throw us into crisis. It is in just such circumstances that our most fundamental beliefs might be revealed as inadequate, and our sense of loss of meaning become overwhelming. And it is in just such circumstances that we might be thrown back into considering the kind of question that Alfie came to ask as a result of the crisis in his own life.

In the absence of a critical level of uneasiness or a significant disruption of one's sense of meaningful identity, then, it is unlikely that any of us would even consider the possibility that our fundamental beliefs might be misguided. Even if we were brought up against our ineffectiveness in some aspect of our lives, and it might be thought that we would thus necessarily question ourselves about our assumptions, such an outcome is by no means certain. We might well feel uneasy or frustrated, but nevertheless simply decide to change our methods, or search for a more favorable opportunity. In short, simple discomfort with a given state of affairs does not inevitably lead us to reappraise our objectives, nor to question whether they are misguided.

Let's summarize: if a commitment to change is only likely to result from being aware of costs, and awareness of costs depends on being open to feedback, it's hard to avoid the conclusion that, in the face of a specific suppression of that awareness and with no envisagement of more satisfying possibilities, none of us would be motivated to change.

As we proposed in Chapter Six, when we were considering the theoretically optimal conditions for an accurate appraisal of reality, one kind of program for change could persuasively be derived from a diagnosis of where unfavorable conditions exist, and what would be needed to improve them. In other words, we would simply need to change the environmental circumstances inhibiting our ability to see the world accurately, curtailing our ability to make sense of it, and restricting our potential for action. The optimal general agenda for such a program would thus consist of removing adverse conditions and fostering positive ones. Such a program would, of course, be a *preventive* one. That is, its purpose would be to optimize our ability to encounter the world accurately in the future. It would not deal with erroneous beliefs already held to be true.

I am overstating the case. Becoming aware of the costs of a given state of affairs is one thing; being aware of how far our own beliefs might play a part in precipitating them is quite another. It is one of the ironies of being human, however, that we always seem to be catching up with the consequences of earlier circumstances and decisions. To design a program to counteract the effects of prior adverse conditions or poor decisions would require that we pay attention instead to promoting optimal conditions for a protagonist, group, or institution to *become aware* of those effects, and in particular, their costs; in other words, *very specifically* to affect motive. Although our thinking in Chapter Six is relevant to both cases, we should be clear that while one process is preventive, the other is remedial. The tasks and difficulties encountered in these two different cases will thus unavoidably be very different. The requirements of a program to promote health will be different from those necessary for effective therapy of illness. Since all of us can be thought to be in the middle of our own potential development as well as that of humankind, we would do well to be committed to both.

Have we in fact then already devised a preventive program? I think not. We have simply suggested the principles it should incorporate. Let's see if we can do something similar for a remedial one.

Of course, identifying principles is a far cry from incorporating them into specific practical action. However, ignorance of fundamental principles is almost necessarily a prescription for disaster. Let's try to be as thorough as possible, then, in discovering the principles that should guide us in our efforts to promote remedial change.

Most importantly, we need to recognize that without an awareness of costs, it's unlikely that any of us would seriously question what we already believe. Unfortunately, we are none of us free of the tendency to attribute the incongruities in our experience to any number of spurious causes: to the accidents of circumstance, for example, or to the hostile motivations or faulty beliefs and attitudes of others. Since few of us will look for alternative explanations of what we feel we already understand, this clearly presents a serious difficulty for anyone who aspires to promote deeper understanding. If a protagonist is unaware of incongruities, or has adequate subjective explanations for them, where does that leave the rest of us? How, in short, are *our* motives affected?

There are at least two different factors to be taken into account. We may be profoundly concerned about the costs of closed-mindedness to the protagonist, and we may also be powerfully affected by our awareness of the costs to others. The costs may impinge upon a single other (perhaps ourselves), or upon many others, up to the whole of humankind, and indeed to all life forms. Although our appraisal of such costs will most obviously be affected by the nature of our own interests, it will also—and most importantly—be affected by the degree to which we are able to understand and take account of the whole context in which the costs occur.

*Our appraisal of the nature of costs in any given occasion is thus most powerfully affected by the balance **in ourselves** of contextual off-centered awareness on the one hand, and centric preoccupation on the other.*

Clearly, the context of any action is comprised not only of the basic motives we asserted earlier as being characteristic of all life forms (that is, to survive and procreate). It is also in part comprised of the manner in which such basic motives affect the process of evolution itself.

Our most far-reaching off-centered concern, then, has to do with appraising how individual or group openness or resistance to change bear on our potential as human beings to take stock of our place in the universe, and thus to contribute to its fullest possible realization.

We need to bear in mind, too, that there is a difference in the manner in which continuity and the realization of potential are revealed as factors in motivation, for, in our case, continuity across generations includes the accumulation of conceptually derived knowledge and sensibility, both about the whole of physical reality (that is, the realm of science) and about the nature of reality itself (that is, the realm of philosophy). Our continuity is thus a continuity of development of civilization and culture, with all the extraordinary extensions of sensibility about the relations between ourselves, other forms of life, and the rest of the universe that can play a part in determining our evolutionary trajectory. The behavior of every individual human being can thus be thought of as contributing to this evolutionary development, as being largely irrelevant to it, or as actively detracting from it. The most serious detractions are those that result from the inhibiting of individual persons from realizing as fully as possible the potential of their own nature, for the presence of inhibitions significantly affects whether that person can contribute something of their own self to our common future.

In the light of this, how can we arrive at a fair assessment of what degree of responsibility each of us has in relation to one another, and thus to the trajectory of humankind? What, in short, is required of any individual one of us to fully realize the meaning of our own existence? What sorts of purposes are practicable for each of us?

What kinds are amenable to cooperative action? Reverting to Donne's insight, we could perhaps ask, too, what responsibility does each of us have in relation to a larger fellowship? It would be a dreadful loss to us all if we were to await the passing bell before becoming actively aware of our belonging to the main. It may be difficult for most of us to imagine, but it is likely, too, that the main to which we belong is, in fact, immeasurably larger than most of us can at the moment comfortably envisage.

Given that, aware or not, we all do belong to a main that at the moment transcends our ability to envisage it, let us try to identify the factors that together might determine whether we can, individually or collectively, and in our continuously developing present, be motivated to change faulty assumptions about the nature of reality.

We've already noted that in the absence of awareness of costs, there can be no motivation for such a change. We could equally well note, however, that an absence of aspiration has a similar effect. Let us summarize this state of affairs somewhat more positively.

If any of us has enough concern or distress about a given state of affairs, and enough hope that such matters can be changed, then we will try to change them.

We could further assert that too much pain or distress can lead to despair (the very word means "without hope"), and that unrealistic ("magical") hope lacks staying power as a motivating force. What is necessary for change, then, seems to be enough uneasiness (but not too much) and enough hope (but of the realistic, rather than the self-deceptive variety). In a series of investigations carried out at the University of Chicago some fifty years ago, this particular balance of factors in the people studied was indeed found to be associated with both a positive engagement in attempts to change, and with satisfactory outcomes. That is, in cases where both positive engagement and actual ameliorative change occurred, this particular balance of hope and discomfort was more likely to have been present.[1]

What can we deduce further from such findings? Let's first summarize them as a series of aphorisms. Thus:

– People who experience little distress about what they believe are unlikely to want change. For such a person, it is unlikely that any change can occur insofar as their own motives are concerned unless they become more uncomfortable; are able to experience the costs attendant upon what they believe, and further, to acknowledge the degree of their own responsibility for them.

– People who experience distress beyond a critical level feel overwhelmed and unable to galvanize themselves into effective action. For such people, it is unlikely that there can be any change as far as their own motives are concerned unless they can become more hopeful. The potential for hope, though, may critically depend on whether change can be effected in a person's external circumstances. The power to do so is not always individually available to us. In such cases, concerted action can be an effective alternative. In some cases it may be the only effective course possible.

– People who have unrealistic expectations of success persistently fail to commit themselves to doing what is necessary to bring about change, even if they consciously believe they desire it. If we believe that success in life depends more on circumstance and providence than on our own efforts, not only may we underestimate the amount of effort needed to bring about change, but we may also fail to understand what kind of effort is necessary. (It also bears saying that our definition of the meaning of the word "success" might itself be a contributory factor in such a case.)

Even if the achievement of optimal circumstantial conditions for
a true encounter with the world presents little theoretical difficulty
(although its realization may present enormous practical ones), the
same cannot be said for the fostering of optimal motives. It may
be possible—even highly probable—that people of widely different
life experiences can agree about what the physical and circumstantial impediments to self-fulfillment are. It is much more difficult
to envisage how individual people, groups, institutions, nations, or
humankind itself can modify what we want and are prepared to
do, whether for ourselves or others: in short, what kind of balance
of costs against gains are any of us likely to be motivated by as we
take account of our relationships with others? In the sensibility of
any such protagonist, then, we are concerned with the balance of
centric preoccupation and off-centered awareness. Critical is the
degree to which we associate our own fulfillment with the fulfillment of our kind, or dissociate it. Do we recognize or deny, honor
or dishonor our interdependence with other lives and other life?
Do we, in short, see others as competing with us for very survival,
or as fellows in the common endeavor of human existence?

It is not difficult, however, to map out how motives affect our
behavior. People (and institutions too) pursue their interests with
a persistence that is determined by the degree to which their experiences seem to validate those interests, and by their sense of how
effective they are in pursuing them. Both depend on the ability to
be open to feedback.

What factor most affects our ability to register accurately the
nature of the feedback we receive about our manner of being
in the world? We've already suggested the nature of the answer.
It depends on the ramifications of the definition we proposed
earlier for one's sense of identity. We asserted that one's sense of
self depends on where we experience the boundary between self
and other to be. We also noted that a characteristic mode of
protection against dissonant feedback from the world is to
disown problematic aspects of our own beliefs, specifically by
attributing the problematic bits to people or forces we experience

as alien to us, *outside* ourselves. This frequently results in our *disempowerment* of ourselves. Figure Two displayed the different possibilities available to us with regard to ownership or projection of responsibility. We can summarize the most important implication of those distinctions in the following way.

*If we are protecting what we believe about ourselves from dissonant feedback, the "self" we are defending seems to find it easier to believe that the dissonance we experience is due, not to something in ourselves, but rather to something **for which we ourselves bear no responsibility**. This is not to deny, however, the complexities we encounter upon recognizing that, on occasion, any of us may actually be right.*

The evidence for the pervasiveness of this mode of thinking among human beings is found, not only in the obvious practical examples of polarized thought and attitudes in politics and international affairs, but also in the more everyday habits of speech. If we are suddenly surprised by some aspect of our own behavior or experience, we say, "I don't know what got into me." If surprised by unfamiliar behavior in someone of our close acquaintance, we exclaim, "She's not herself today." Further, when in exasperation we burst out with "Whose side are you on?" we are simply paraphrasing the thought "Are you a participant member of our continuity of belief, or of someone else's?" (in short, an *outside* enemy). President Nixon found it impossible to think of those who opposed the war in Vietnam as being true Americans.

There are many ways to draw a line between ourselves and others—indeed, between ourselves and *everything else*. Notwithstanding these variations, it is clear that the ultimate expression by human beings of our alienation from others of our own kind is our characterization of those others as *not truly human*.

The central dynamic of these processes is, of course, dissociating ourselves from identity with others. If we do not resort to dissociation, but instead recognize some kind of association with others, we are recognizing a commonality that places us under a different kind of obligation to ourselves and to others at the same time. If we can declare, as the cartoon character did, "We have met the enemy, and he is us,"[2] then we have to deal with ourselves, and others as a part of ourselves: in short, with all of us together as members of humankind. If we do so, we are obviously concentrating on what is problematic. Let us not lose sight, then, of the omitted factor: "We have met our ally, and our ally is also us."[3]

It is important, in the light of the pervasiveness of associative and dissociative processes, that we seriously take them into account when attempting to motivate for change those who are ignorant of—or have little concern for—the harmful consequences of their beliefs. If we want to influence the motives of others, we necessarily have to deal with the dilemma represented by the distinction between self and other, since anyone attempting to make a difference to the beliefs of others is necessarily an other to *them*.

The presence of a dissociative element in attempts to produce change can be tellingly illustrated, even epitomized, in the following (somewhat trenchant) expressions of it.

"Shock the Burghers!" [That was the French poet Charles Baudelaire's rallying cry to the disaffected in late nineteenth-century Paris.[4]]

"It is good for people to be shocked; indeed, it is important for them to be shocked fairly often." [This one, somewhat more measured, is due to George Bernard Shaw.[5]]

"When in Rome, do as the Greeks!"[6] [I couldn't resist adding this tongue-in-cheek variant, which comes from Kenneth Burke.]

The shared underlying justification for such recommendations can be found in the assumptions we have made about how we understand the physical world: namely, by learning from the discrepancies between our expectations of physical reality and our direct experience of it. In contrast to what we have come to accept as characteristic of primitive human thought (where natural physical events are attributed to the motives of supernatural beings of some kind), modern human beings have for the most part come to accept that the natural world works according to inexorable physical laws, so there is little psychological need to postulate motive in one's environment, except in the kind of circumstances we described earlier. In the normal course of events, incongruities arising in our experience of the purely physical world may evoke concerns about survival or opportunity, but rarely of identity. Incongruities encountered in our experience of physical reality tend to be dealt with in a very practical manner: dangers are avoided; opportunities are seized. Actions that do not yield the anticipated result are modified according to circumstance until they yield a sufficiently successful outcome. Beyond such practical considerations, it is nevertheless true that human beings will also attempt to fit particular physical environmental events into the overall explanatory schemes we have devised for understanding natural phenomena. In the main, however, physical phenomena that cause uncomfortable discrepancies for such conceptual schemes are rare. They tend rather to be a feature of the experience of specialized scientific investigators than of people going about everyday lives.

How are these considerations relevant to anyone who is attempting to give a protagonist a different perspective on their primary frame beliefs? The assumption that symbolically mediated feedback will be met by a protagonist with the same kind of mindset as simple physical, non-mediated experience is clearly faulty. A protagonist may not respond to an interlocutor's activity as neutral, but as more likely to be biased by that person's own values and interests. In short, such a protagonist will be suspicious of the interlocutor's motives, and will primarily be concerned to know whether he or she stands as an ally or as an enemy.

This kind of concern, in the case of a burgher being shocked by the posturing of a dandified poet, or an audience with conventional beliefs being shocked by the polemic of a free-thinking playwright, would be unlikely to result, I think, in capitulation to some new standard of belief. It doesn't seem very probable, either, that Romans shocked by Greeks are likely to run to the local library and start perusing Plato's *Dialogues*.

The major difficulty of this differentiating, dissociating approach, then, is that it contributes to the creation of a symmetrical collusion. The motives attributed to any interlocutor by any protagonist will tend to be those that affirm the primary frame beliefs of both. Being shocked fairly often is not a very useful overall program for producing change, then, if the nature of the shock depends on the self-justifying, (self-dissociating) motives of the shocker. We cannot easily find common cause with those who strike alienating postures under the illusion that they are fostering new kinds of awareness. Unfortunately, a shocker who parades his own sense of alienation from the targeted person or group necessarily (but possibly unknowingly) *promotes* the targeted person's alienation from him. Strident dissonances and defiant attitudes may well serve an affirmative identity-purpose for enclaves of frustrated, self-styled intellectual revolutionaries, but increased open-mindedness on the part of society as a whole is unlikely to follow. Obviously, self-serving shock tactics not only do not produce self-examination on the part of the target-person or group, they also provide that person or group with a readily available reason for attributing alienating motives to their interlocutor. Such perceived motives lend themselves well to being classified according to readily available junk-terms. Even in the case of less belligerent motives— as with Greeks fortuitously in the streets of Rome—the word "foreign" is readily available to quickly and easily assign Greek sensibility to the junk heap. *No change* is the result.

The plain fact is that an incongruity in experience must be of such a type that it not only calls into question some aspect of one's prior organization of reality, but also cannot be easily disposed of by being attributed to the self-serving interests of some interlocutor for whom one already has available a number of suitable junk-terms. Shocks for which one's propositions already have explanations simply don't produce a sufficient challenge to established belief.

We've already argued, too, that most people cannot sustain uncertainty for very long, so that, in the face of a recognized incongruity of experience, change is much more likely to come about if an alternative hypothesis of explanation is waiting in the wings. Interestingly, George Orwell, who gave considerable thought to the manner in which people can be persuaded to modify their fundamental propositions about the world, came to believe that Shaw was able to shock people so successfully because the seeds of personal doubt had already taken root in the minds of his audiences, and they were therefore ripe for different formulations.[7] It's possible, too, of course, that for most people, going to the theatre is a kind of "time out" that enables them to be more objective about themselves, *without* the pressure for immediate decision-making that is usually an ever-present feature of our lives. It is possible, undoubtedly, that one could assign some self-serving motive to the playwright, particularly if the play were blatantly polemical, but the fiction itself would (if powerful) give the illusion of a reality at some remove from the immediate preoccupations of an audience. In such circumstances, perhaps, as we observe fictional others living out their beliefs in fictional life-space, we are more easily able to see ourselves. Accordingly the theatre may be thought of as almost a kind of workshop for the development of off-centered sensibility. It may not *instruct* us in how to be different, but it can enable us to meditate on what could happen if we were.

The theatre can give us the opportunity for an outside perspective on our own lives, then, without the tendency (common in other circumstances) to reject almost instinctively formulations of reality that conflict with our own.

Orwell's comments can, moreover, open up another set of possibilities which have long been well-known to students of rhetoric. Rhetoric is, of course, the study and practice of the art of verbal persuasion. Aristotle, Cicero, and more recently Burke, Northrop Frye, and undoubtedly many others, have pointed to the necessity in rhetoric of claiming and giving evidence (possibly spurious, of course) of some shared identity on the part of the aspiring persuader and an audience. We are here touching on the presence of an associative element: namely, one that emphasizes the *fellowship* of the participants by inviting their participation in affirming a critical fundamental belief, whether it pertains to a particular circumstance or to a more general issue.

Rhetoric, however, is not for the most part concerned with the establishment of truth, but rather with the influencing of opinion to serve the objectives of the aspiring persuader. For the hopeful persuader, there is necessarily what we might call a "program" for a solution to the uncertainty that the audience is presumed to have, or that it can be persuaded to have. Whatever the case, the persuader's technique is to proclaim, "We are in this together. I feel as you feel, I aspire as you aspire, I suffer as you suffer." (Adolf Hitler, I must add, was a consummate master of the technique.) The appeal is thus to a kind of solidarity of basic belief, and therefore identity. Frye summarizes it succinctly:

> The principle invoked is that we belong to something *before* we are anything, that our loyalties and sense of solidarity are *prior* to intelligence."[8] [My emphasis.]

Frye makes the case, very relevant to our own concerns, that, although according to Aristotle's ideal, rhetoric should be at the service of the dialectic[9] (read "objective search for truth via the comparison of different perspectives"), in practice, in the rhetorical situation "at its worst," there is a deliberate attempt to put the watchdog of consciousness to sleep. "For a mob," says Frye, "the kind of independent judgment appealed to by dialectic is an act of open defiance, and is normally treated as such."[10] Dialectic, in short, requires the exercising of an objective intelligence, an off-centered awareness, which is fundamentally *associative*. Such an awareness is in logical opposition to that widely favored rhetorical technique, the argument *ad hominem* (as, for example, in: "You're only saying that because you want my job!"), whose purpose, as Frye points out, is simply to stop logical argument altogether. The ad hominem argument is simply a manifestation of the rhetorician's willingness to use dissociative methods to avoid engagement in dialectic itself. An experienced rhetorician can switch from associative to dissociative modes with virtuoso ease. That this can be done so convincingly is usually indicative that the appeal to solidarity of identity has already implied the existence of a common enemy.

We've already noted how the identification of a common enemy can foster the group solidarity of those who experience themselves as being inside a metaphorical protective circle of wagons. What we should also note is that rhetoric fosters this kind of polarity. The watchdog of consciousness is, in contrast, one that weighs and allows for the persuasiveness of different perspectives. It is *off-centered*. Inside the wagons, *and* outside? Yes, indeed.

We must be watchful, however, lest we ourselves become smug about the ease with which we can all call to mind examples of rhetorical manipulations of opinion *by others*. (Do we ourselves use such ploys? Of course not!) One could make a strong case, for example, that modern democratic processes are strongly marked, particularly in the periods before elections, by blatantly flourished polarized thinking. The parties to such rhetorical practices may be thought of, I think, as sharing common assumptions about adversary-ness that prevent their admitting to personal uncertainty or ambivalence. In our present political arenas, woe betides the politician who is willing to admit to either.[11]

It is probably a mistake, however, to condemn the various techniques of rhetoric in a single lump; after all, Frye himself was a superior exponent of many of them, and, for anyone who is acquainted with Frye's conspicuously searching writing, his commitment to truth can scarcely be doubted. Although we may

agree with Aristotle that the pursuit of truth is morally superior
to rhetoric, we would have to concede, as Frye himself does, that
"rhetoric expresses and appeals to a more comprehensive enlist-
ing of the personality than simple argument."[12] Our problem,
then, is that dialectic alone does not usually trigger the emotional
charge and energy that may be necessary to break up a logjam
of erroneous belief. A potential agent of change needs something
stronger, something that can ignite what we tend to speak
of metaphorically as a flash of insight, a revelation: in short,
something that has the power "to strike with astonishment."[13]

Words are of course only one mode of representation, and it
may well be that although they may present something that is
beyond them, the critical factor for effecting change may occur
more powerfully when it is not mediated by words, but appears
directly.

Yet again, it is Orwell's comment on Shaw's aphorism that yields
a credible suggestion as to the nature of that critical factor. It is the
entire context of verbal exchange, in addition to the words themselves, that contributes to or detracts from their power to produce
an effect. Orwell himself illustrated this convincingly, both in
Animal Farm and in *1984*. It is tempting to suggest that words,
because they are no more than abstract representations, can never
have an impact that matches the one afforded by direct experience,
at least insofar as bringing about a questioning of fundamental
beliefs is concerned. All of us, however, will have had experiences
that convincingly refute such a hypothesis. Words may not be able
to match the physical or emotional impact of direct experience,
but they have extraordinary power to promote understanding, or
to sabotage it (as, in fact, Orwell goes to considerable pains to
show). The question is, what kinds of context enable them to do
so? What combination of direct experience and mediated experience is necessary to foster both the right kind of uneasiness about
what one believes, and the right kind of confidence that a better
mode of understanding is possible?

In our earlier discussion of the nature of off-centered awareness, we commented on its being characterized by the ability to not only observe ourselves as if from the outside, but also to understand the perspective of others by projecting our own sensibility imaginatively into theirs. Off-centeredness, in fact, is an ability that contains both the power to experience, as if from within, the identity of another, and from without, the identity of ourselves. What is more, a strong case could be made that either perspective strengthens the acuity of the other.

We also noted earlier that such an observing awareness is more likely to operate when we are not deeply preoccupied with some demanding task, nor feeling under threat, regardless of whether that threat is symbolic or actual. We spoke, too, of the kind of circumstance in which we are capable of being sufficiently open-minded to entertain thoughts of possible change. In particular, it was clear that we would give adequate weight to incongruities in experience if those incongruities became evident as a result of our own effort to discern them. An incongruity encountered as a result of one's own exploratory activity would have the quality of affirming identity, rather than threatening it, because it would be an indicator, not of one's inadequacy, but rather of one's effectiveness. Creative growth and indeed any advancement of understanding are most likely to occur for us when we are actively seeking to realize—that is, fulfill—our own being, rather than protect it.

The prototype anecdote that illustrates the principle involved is told, with typical verve and flourish, by the writer G. K. Chesterton. In his autobiography, Chesterton tells of his response to a visitor who had arrived unexpectedly at his home in Battersea, London, where Chesterton and his wife were busily completing their packing in preparation for a trip abroad. The visitor, noticing that the various articles of luggage sported labels indicating a number of different destinations in Europe, naturally asked the Chestertons where they were going. "Why, to Battersea!" exclaimed the author (gleefully enjoying, I am sure, his questioner's puzzlement).

Chesterton's eventual full explanation was that it was only after visiting a succession of contrasting places in Europe that he would be able briefly, truly to see his own home, which he had become too familiar with to experience accurately.

Not all of us are as conscientious as Chesterton claims to have been in exposing ourselves to new experiences that might throw us temporarily off our usual balance. It is likely, however, that most of us, at some time or other, have had the experience (*unplanned*) of suddenly being confronted with an event or circumstance that did not simply shatter an earlier belief, but also revealed with a kind of blinding certainty that a totally new way of understanding had opened before us. We have only clumsy and inadequate verbal summaries available for such moments:

"It was as if my whole world had suddenly turned upside down!"

"I felt as if I'd been struck by lightning!"

Upon considering what is common here, we are likely to find that, like Shaw's audiences, some part of us was already primed and ready for the revelation, even if (unlike Chesterton) we had not planned to foster its occurrence. It is unlikely, of course, that the insights brought about by Chesterton's return to England would have been as dramatic, but he was clearly familiar with such moments, and had not only identified the nature of the circumstances that were likely to produce them, but also was consciously contributing to their realization. Those circumstances all give evidence of a similar principle at work:

The protagonist is suddenly aware of a different perspective on events, one that transforms what was familiar but inadequately understood, to something that, because of sudden unfamiliarity, can be seen truly, without the set of accumulated assumptions that had previously worked to hide its true nature.

The actual dynamic of this mode of encounter—coming across something as if for the first time—is crucially characterized by the essential quality of off-centeredness, of coming at *oneself* as if from the outside; in other words, taking an observer status in relation to what was previously not observed, but experienced from within, centrically. This dynamic is also exactly that which characterizes the ability to laugh at ourselves. To laugh at ourselves requires that we be imaginatively outside, looking in: outside, but *not* dissociated. It can best be characterized, perhaps, as being able to have a *sympathetic* understanding of ourselves and what is incongruent in us. When we can do so, we are not *immersed* in ourselves, but are rather aware of ourselves *in our context*.

In sum: to experience the irony of our own incongruity itself contains the essential element of what is critical for change.

It is important—*crucially* important—however, that we not confuse our ability to laugh at ourselves with the apparently similar ability to laugh at others. It is possible, of course, to laugh *with* others at themselves, just as others may laugh *with us* at ourselves, because such activity is also sympathetic and associative. To laugh at another because of their apparent difference from ourselves is, by contrast, *dissociative* (at Greeks on the street in Rome, for example), and simply reinforces our adherence to the particular continuity of belief that emphasizes our difference from others, and thus, by implication, our superiority over them.

To transform the familiar into the unfamiliar ("making the familiar strange") is a technique that has long been known to poets, dramatists, and novelists. The poet Shelley considered it to be the very essence of poetry.[14] The playwright Bertolt Brecht considered it to be the dominant element in great drama.[15]

The formalist critic Viktor Shklovsky considered it to be the distinguishing feature of great prose, and persuasively documented its force in the works of Leo Tolstoi.[16] We might suggest, too, that the very designation "novel" registers its significance for that particular literary form.

Again, however, we must not jump to easy conclusions, however undoubtedly desirable they might be. It doesn't do to assign to any particular technique the magic "Open Sesame!" to the door of change. As we discerned earlier, it is not simply the quality of a particular event, nor the surrounding circumstances, that affect our ability to encounter it. It is also the very specific nature of our abilities, both perceptual and cognitive, as well as the nature of the sense of identity that is being defended. All these factors interact in very complex ways. It follows, then, that for anyone attempting to contribute to positive change, discerning specifically what is preventing protagonists from being aware of the shortcomings of their understanding may be of crucial importance, since each unfavorable factor may require a different mode of resolution, depending on the character of the error, or the circumstances fostering it. Actually discerning what those obstacles are might itself prove to be a major enterprise.

Clearly, there are two fundamental ways in which one can encounter an incongruity. One can fail to recognize that an incongruity exists, or one can recognize that it does. If the protagonist does not register an incongruity, the possibilities are:

- Optimal perceptual circumstances do not exist.

- The protagonist may have his/her attention directed elsewhere.

- The protagonist's conceptual inventory is insufficient for a more complete understanding of the situation.

Clearly, too, in each of these circumstances, the protagonist is in no position to be able to appraise the costs of the incongruity, and thus will have none of the motivating discomfort that is necessary for change.

If an incongruity is in fact registered by the protagonist, the following possibilities are conceivable:

- The protagonist is aware of the incongruity, but unaware of its costs.

- The protagonist is aware of the incongruity, appraises its costs inadequately, and consequently decides to disregard them.

- The protagonist is aware of the incongruity, appraises its costs accurately, and is prepared to pay them in order to achieve some other advantage.

- The protagonist is aware of the incongruity, appraises its costs accurately, is reluctant to pay them, but cannot think of any better mode of action.

- The protagonist is aware of the incongruity, appraises its costs accurately, and undertakes to find a solution.

Each of these possibilities immediately indicates what would be required for its resolution, or at least the primary factors to be taken into account. Of course, there is much complexity involved in how that can actually be done, and more than can be adequately dealt with here. Nevertheless the character of those endeavors should be clear:

- If optimal perceptual conditions do not exist, they will need to be fostered.

– If the protagonist's attention is elsewhere, it will need to be redirected.

– If the protagonist lacks the concepts that are necessary for a fuller understanding, he or she will need to be helped to consider new conceptualizations.

– If the protagonist lacks sufficient conceptual ability, some way must be found to translate the reality of his or her situation or behavior into terms that are already available. Alternatively, it may be possible for the protagonist to be accessible to some kind of direct experience that brings the situation home (and that's a really significant word!) in a manner more accessible to his or her particular sensibility.[17]

– If the protagonist registers the incongruity, but is unaware of the costs of the behavior that produced it, evidence of costs will need to be provided. Simple information may be sufficient, but if it is not, an interlocutor's activity will need to be directed by the considerations that apply in our subsequent examples.

– If the protagonist is aware of some costs but not others, he or she will need to be exposed to the evidence of other costs.

– If the protagonist appraises the costs accurately, but is prepared to accept them in order to achieve some other advantage, he or she must be helped to reappraise the balance of costs against gains. If, however, the costs are felt by others, and not by the protagonist, an interlocutor may be faced with a situation to which we have already referred; that is, one where a protagonist, for purely centric reasons, has no concern about the costs to others, and may indeed precipitate those costs in order to achieve a competitive advantage. Paulo Freire[18] has suggested, however, that the protagonist's interests in such a case are not to his benefit. The reality is that the protagonist who thinks only of personal benefit and disregards the costs to others, or even engineers them is, in fact, misrepresenting the situation. The protagonist is unaware of the costs to him- or herself.

This last situation is obviously critical for the survival and development of humankind, since it epitomizes the difference between the workings of centric sensibility on the one hand, and a contextually aware, off-centered sensibility on the other. Freire's suggested solution was for a determined commitment to the broadest possible educational program for oppressed and oppressors alike, namely, one that would promote awareness of our common responsibilities and obligations to one another. Realizing our potential as a species may well depend on the degree to which we can afford that opportunity to all of us.

Such a program clearly cannot result from anything other than a connected awareness of the difficulties facing us. We are speaking, then, of the optimal kind of off-centered response to those of us whose sense of being-in-the-world is pervasively centric. Our first necessity must be to avoid allowing our own centric preoccupations to reverberate destructively with those of others.

In short, as potential agents of change, our first responsibility is not to collude in protecting the continuity of faulty belief of a protagonist, whether person or institution, nor participate in the harmful modes of interaction they promote. Nor must we find convenient junk-terms to reassure ourselves. If we are to foster the opportunities that could lead to positive change, we must neither fudge nor disregard the similarities and differences between us.

We must, however, not underestimate the difficulty we are likely to face in attempting to associate productively with any protagonist with centric preoccupations. Such protagonists may have no pressing need to remain in any kind of communicative context with an interlocutor, because continued (dialectical) contact does not serve their continuity of belief.

In any human society, then, for anyone attempting to produce change in another's primary frame beliefs (and that may include the conventional prevailing primary frame beliefs of the societies in which we all live) the major decision has to do with how significant any particular adherence to faulty beliefs is considered to be, what kind of productive dissonance can be produced for anyone who maintains such beliefs, and what kind of circumstances would enable us to do so. Of course, no single person can take on in its entirety the mass of issues facing humanity, but we all have an investment in those issues being faced. In particular, it seems crucial that we do not despair of the possibility of change, and thus withdraw from efforts to foster it. We have all met up with despairing junk aphorisms like "People will never change," or "No individual can make a difference." There may be times, in fact, when we ourselves entertain such ideas. Our history as a species refutes such assertions, however. People have always changed, and individuals have always made a significant difference.

It is a gross oversimplification, of course, for any of us to consider that the protagonists in a situation are always others, and not ourselves. Off-centeredness is a marvelous attribute, but none of us is ever a completely objective observer. We are all protagonists, and all potential agents for change in relation to one another. We all, willy-nilly, contribute to the potential realization of humankind, or detract from it. We are in this together.

Still, what is it that we are actually "in" together? It's time to give that larger question the attention it deserves.

10

A Better Question—and an Answer

OUR UNDERTAKING thus far has been to investigate how the way we make sense affects the kind of sense we are able to make.

It's important to remind ourselves once more, then, that, in returning to the kind of ultimate questions we specifically deferred answering at the outset, it is our manner of making sense that predetermines the kinds of propositions that qualify as viable answers to them.

Accordingly, in returning to a consideration of Alfie's question, we must ask ourselves once more—and this time even more specifically than we have thus far—*how* he and we have come to ask it in that particular way. In so doing, we may well find, not only a different form for the question, but a different set of possibilities for the answer.

Readers who are familiar with the original play or the first movie version of *Alfie* will remember that "What's it all about?" is the question that marks Alfie's sudden and shattering revelation that his life has been lived as if his interests alone were the only significant factors in his existence. His realization that he is a part of something that had previously not existed for him represents a dramatic awakening of his awareness of himself as a self. As we have previously argued, the awareness of oneself *as a self* is the necessary condition, not only for recognizing the subjective reality of other selves, but also for discerning how each subjective self deals with the reality of everything else. That is what off-centeredness means. A centrically motivated being cannot ask Alfie's question.

Alfie's story, then, is a prototype. It is the story of one person's dramatic shift from an unselfconscious pursuit of centrically determined personal objectives to a potentially sympathetic awareness of the existential claims of others. That is, it is a shift from a *dissociative* competitive mode to the possibility of an *associative* cooperative one. We can attribute the power of the dramatist's portrayal of that shift directly to his skill in showing us the elements of that transition, and also in providing a triggering event that seizes us by the throat. What we need to take specific note of, however, is that neither for Alfie nor for us does symbolic ability lead inevitably to an awareness of other perspectives. It is, rather, the essential prior condition. It creates the opportunity for the realization of off-centered awareness, *but only if other factors are favorable.*

For me, there is in the very form of Alfie's question a sense of the despair of ever finding an answer. It is a despair that in our darkest moments finds its sympathetic vibration in all of us. Alfie suddenly discovers that his life has been lived without any significant regard for the interests of others. The hermetic boundary he had devised for himself is starting to disintegrate. A case could be made that we, too, are as a species only just beginning to come to terms with the idea that human beings throughout history have been both ignorantly and at times systematically inattentive to the nature of our impact not only on other creatures and our natural environment, but also on one another.

In fact, even though the emergence in humanity of symbolizing mental activity represents a watershed in evolution, its potential for the development of a truly objective but nevertheless engaged intelligence, one that is not at the mercy of purely instinctive motives, nor in disregard of our obligations to other existence, is only *in process* of being realized. I use the word "watershed" in order to give adequate weight to the enormity of the difference between a life-universe consisting of centrically motivated life forms preoccupied primarily with survival, and one which (possibly for the first time) includes forms that have the ability to appraise their own position in relation to other forms, and thus to see their own significance in the process of evolution itself.

It is quite likely, I think, that the emergence of an off-centered intelligence constitutes as important an event in the evolution of the universe as the emergence of life itself.

I am suggesting, of course, that we as a species are in a position in relation to ourselves that is directly analogous to Alfie's newly experienced awareness of himself. His question doesn't simply accidentally resemble ours. It contains similar fundamental assumptions. Alfie is at the very beginning of transcending his own centricity. Why, then, does he not ask, "What am I about?" rather than "What is it about?" This latter question, which is also ours, is a dissociative one. It is certainly off-centered, in that it looks beyond the perceiving self, but it is also disqualifying of that perceiving self. In short, it omits the questioning self from the question. Whatever the *it* is, it apparently excludes the questioner. Whatever the *it* is, the questioner assumes that he or she is passive, and therefore inactive in relation to that *it*, rather than part of what makes that *it* what it is.

I am in fact declaring that when we ask the question in the same form as Alfie, we are similarly disqualifying and dissociating ourselves from the *it* we are so eager to understand. The form of the question already implies that we are excluded from any effective role in answering it.

The reason for this sudden exclusion of self, I think, is similar in the case of both Alfie and ourselves. Alfie is still staggering from the overwhelming implications of his realization that other people may have claims on existence that are no less significant than his own. Previously, he had experienced only the certainty of his centricity. He now has to face the uncertainty and questioning to which a wider connected awareness gives rise. It is not surprising, then, that he should be temporarily lost to himself, nor that his jump to the largest question of all should exclude himself. Like the finally self-conscious "outsider" who is the protagonist in Albert Camus' novel *L'Etranger,* it is as if Alfie is suddenly all but overwhelmed by an awareness of his loneliness, the previously suppressed cost of his own disconnectedness from others.[1] It is too early for him to be able to realize that there can be a place for him in existence that does not require that he be solely occupied with himself.

I think something similar is being experienced in the large by humankind. Our cumulative experience over millennia can be seen as leading to a questioning of ourselves that is equivalent to Alfie's questioning of himself. Each of us is individually confronted every day with the evidence that, as a species, we have not yet come fully to terms with our disregard of one another, let alone of everything else. It is apparently easier to contemplate an *it* we do not understand, than an *I* or a *we* that defies our comprehension.

Possibly Alfie's question does not *require* that we be excluded from its answer, but its form does reflect the implication that we should be looking for an answer that is not only beyond ourselves, *outside ourselves,* but also assumes some "larger" purposeful agent. As we argued in the earlier chapters, our experience of purpose in ourselves and other creatures almost inexorably persuades us of the probability of a supreme agent, a "final cause." Indeed, our very conceptualization of purpose itself contains the assumption that ends determine any activity whatsoever. Our mindset tells us that this must be as true for the universe as it is for us. We rarely in our everyday activities question ourselves about *our* purposes, because they seem to emerge inexorably from the hurly-burly of normal living. However, if we could conjecture some universal purpose, some final cause, which (regardless of actual evidence) could be experienced as relevant to our own motives and preoccupations, then we would be able to see ourselves as living meaningful lives. If, on the other hand, our conjectures were to founder upon the incomprehensibility of that cause, and lead us to the conclusion that our own motives and preoccupations were irrelevant to its potential fulfillment, then our own lives would, in the overall context of existence, be rendered meaningless.

Experiencing ourselves as meaningless (i.e., effectively *useless*) is our ultimate horror. We do not want to live our lives for nothing. We want our lives to have a direction and a purpose, because we want our lives to be relevant to something *beyond* our simple survival.[2] It is understandable, then, that so many of us should devise or subscribe to schemes that provide us with a sense of connectedness to some ultimate purpose. It is also understandable that, in the face of feedback from the world that is incongruent with such schemes, their adherents postulate some presumed higher understanding that is in the purview only of a God. By definition, such an understanding, since it is not available to mere mortals, must be accepted on faith. Hence the widespread appeal to faith in order to deny significance to any experience that is incompatible with the fictional absolute to which one is committed.

As we have seen, however, the fictions to which we may be committed are not always religious ones. The assumptions contained in our conceptualizations, and the propositions permitted by them, can be espoused with little reservation, even if those assumptions promote frequent incongruities between expectation and outcome. We can, in fact, become as habituated to a particular method, a way of acting in the world, as we may be to a particular factual belief.

Is there a better alternative? Indeed there is.

The philosopher Paul Feyerabend once remarked refreshingly that the optimal scientific method could be succinctly summarized as simply doing one's damnedest.[3] If we are to make better sense, doing our damnedest is not a bad summary, it seems to me, of what we—humankind—need to be committed to. I am suggesting, in fact, that this is a higher and more useful moral commitment than any that relies on the manufacture of junk-terms (like an anthropomorphic God, for example, or Heaven, or Hell) to substitute fictional beliefs for a true encounter with the uncertainty that can lead us to a wider understanding. It isn't only religions, however, that offer the opportunity for withdrawal from a full human engagement with the reality of our existential situation. In particular, for many, the methods of science seem to emphasize both the universe's aloofness from us, and the irrelevance of our personal concerns to its unfolding. For large numbers of humanity, the wonder of physical existence alone is insufficient to afford the sense of attachment to ultimate purpose that we so powerfully yearn for.

What would constitute an engagement with our situation that neither denies that yearning nor dismisses its relevance? Well, in brief, an engagement that begins with the question that both Alfie and we ourselves have been pulling back from: "What are *we* about?"

Aha! We are now a significant part of the reality we are trying to understand! We are back *inside* a question that recognizes the reality that we have an active part to play in its answer. We might perhaps ask also something like "What role do we have to play in the universe?" for clearly, we *do* play a part in it. These questions are not only expressive of an off-centered observing awareness, but they also presume a connectedness between the questioner and all other questioners, and a connectedness with everything that is.

The power in such questions is that they are *associative* rather than *dissociative*. Asking them specifically excludes the kind of answer that has any of us simply strutting our hour upon the stage, with our roles already written for us, our destinies solely described by our eventual disappearance into the oblivion of the wings. They all offer the possibility of a viable answer, since they recognize that, because we are consciously able to choose the direction, not only of our own lives, but also of our communal life, our aspirations can affect the future possibilities of life itself.

In that associative spirit, let me attempt an answer for your, and our, consideration. Thus:

We are a part of the evolutionary process of the universe. In us is expressed, possibly for the first time, a new element in that process. That new element is an awareness of the working of the universe and of ourselves, and a critical ability to examine our own worth as contributors to, or detractors from, the evolutionary process itself. Our individual minds, and our common cooperative mind, represent that aspect of Nature that can contemplate, examine, and take stock of itself. We don't simply live out our hour upon the stage. Quite the contrary. We are *involved* in the writing of the continuous drama of life. Our possibilities for contributing to the progress of that drama are beyond our current ability to determine, although some part of them may be envisaged. What we do to and with ourselves and our world has a potentially critical significance for the future course of Nature, of whose self-observing mind, we must avow, we are at the moment possibly only the very slender beginning. Nevertheless, we together constitute an *awesomely* exceptional development in the evolution of all that exists. We have yet to recognize the power and potential of off-centered observing, appraising awareness to affect the course of evolution itself.

Our obligation, then, is to use our understanding to optimize our contribution to the potential for cooperation amongst ourselves, to transcend simple exclusive preoccupation with self, and to foster creativity in any form that bids fair to contribute to evolutionary progress. A significant contribution to that progress is within the power of each of us individually, and all of us in concert. This is a *moral* commitment. It does not require for its fulfillment a specific envisagement of an ultimate consummation, a final "end."

On the contrary, it makes our process our purpose.

That, I believe, is enough for any human lifespan, since our contribution to that process connects us meaningfully with those who have gone before, and those who are yet to come. None of us needs to feel that our individual life is totally circumscribed by its location in space, nor its span in time.

We need to celebrate the extraordinary fortune of being born as a life form that is capable of taking stock of itself, its position and potential future in the cosmos, and its potential relationship with currently inconceivable others. We can celebrate by exercising our powers to the utmost to fulfill the potential of that position.

You may remember that some hundred pages ago, I referred to Kenneth Burke's remark that an analysis of the manner in which we make sense is difficult for us to sustain because the various urgencies of our lives seem to mean that such an enterprise is always off the subject.

*What if, though, it is our very ability to make sense that is itself the subject? In other words, the **fundamental** sense we make together as a species is **the fact that we make it?***

Sense is a function of the way it is made. If we can commit ourselves to improving the way we make it, we will be knowingly engaged in contributing to the realization of the universe itself.

Commentary on the Notes

ALTHOUGH ALL REFERENCES and quotations are documented below, they do not give an adequate picture of my indebtedness to those who have preceded me. What I owe to individuals is chronicled in my separate acknowledgements. This preamble attempts to give an idea of the extent to which I have been influenced by prior writers.

I have been influenced primarily and profoundly by four major writers: Alfred North Whitehead, Ernst Cassirer, Susanne K. Langer, and Kenneth Burke. Their major works are listed in the bibliography, but since those works vary enormously, both in their transparency and their availability, there may be some value in indicating which of them I have found most useful.

Ernst Cassirer's major work, *The Philosophy of Symbolic Forms*, is extensive and exhaustive, but it is in three massive volumes, and few others than readers with specialized concerns are likely to be willing to undertake it. The much later *Essay on Man* is, however, in one short volume, and covers very concisely the same area. Cassirer's erudition is awesome and his sensitive humanity apparent throughout.

The situation is somewhat similar for Whitehead's writing. His *Process and Reality* is his major metaphysical work, but its ideas are more accessibly expressed in *Modes of Thought*, *The Function of Reason*, and *Symbolism: Its Meaning and Effect*.

Adventures of Ideas is a delightful survey of the role of ideas in the development of civilization, which is Whitehead's favorite synonym for the ascent of humankind. It needs to be said, however, that Whitehead's vocabulary, particularly in *Process and Reality,* is likely to present a significant barrier to many readers. In that regard, I have found Elizabeth M. Kraus's *The Metaphysics of Experience* to be particularly helpful.

Susanne Langer, too, is the author of a hefty three-volume opus—*Mind: An Essay on Human Feeling.* Owing to growing blindness, she was unfortunately unable to complete it in the manner she would have wished, but it is a wonderful book, and has been the prime contributory source for my own understanding of the nature of the transition from animal to human sensibility. Langer's most powerful insight was that feeling itself is an aspect of intellect, and should be treated with the respect it deserves. I think the best approach to Langer's thought is via a prior reading of *Philosophy in a New Key,* which establishes the need for that new key with Langer's almost unique combination of intellectual toughness, eloquence, and grace.

What is it possible to say most helpfully about Kenneth Burke? He defies classification, in part perhaps because he most clearly illustrates in his own writing the value of fearlessly shifting around the pieces and combinations of pieces that might lock together into a satisfactory picture of meaning. He is, in short, the least linear of writers, which makes reading him an exciting dance of mingled exasperation and delight. In spite of his enormous influence on others who have preoccupied themselves with the manner in which meaning is created in all aspects of human society, he unfortunately remains little known outside particular areas of specialization. I believe his time is still to come. The best entry into his work, I believe, is via *Permanence and Change.* An excellent brief introduction to his whole body of work appears in the introductory essay by Joseph R. Gusfield in Gusfield's compendium volume *On Symbols and Society,* University Chicago Press, 1989. An extended extract from Gusfield's introductory essay is available on the Internet.

One other writer needs to be singled out for special comment. He is F. S. C. Northrop, whose article "The Importance of Deductively Formulated Theory in Ethics and Social and Legal Science" in *Structure, Method, and Meaning: Essays in Honor of Henry M. Sheffer,* ed. Paul Henle at al., was my own "Open Sesame!" for the approach I have tried to remain faithful to throughout this book.

By and large, the notes that follow are concerned principally with an adequate indication of sources. Here and there, however, I have felt that more needed to be said about the particular significance of those sources to the course of the book's argument. In consequence, I have on occasion tried to deal more fully with matters that would have distracted from the flow if presented in the course of the text itself. There are undoubtedly a few back-eddies still remaining in the text, but the reader who wants to explore those eddies more thoroughly will find them exposed, adequately I hope, in what follows.

Notes

Introduction

1. I am paraphrasing from Kenneth Burke's *Attitudes Towards History,*
page 191.

Chapter One. Alfie: "What's it all about?"

1. I have a reason for introducing Alfie, since we'll return to him more
closely at a later point. I do need to explain, though, that I am referring
to the play and the similarly titled movie in its first version, and not
to the second movie version. The latter movie is a travesty of the
author Bill Naughton's original play. The author himself was however
responsible for the screenplay of the first movie, released in 1966,
which featured Michael Caine in the role of the principal character.
2. I am referring to the second law of thermodynamics. There is a full
discussion of the apparent incongruity of the evolution of life forms
in a "dead" universe at *http:www.entropylaw.com.*

For readers wishing to explore further our understanding of the
processes involved in the evolution of the very earliest of life forms,
it would be hard to do better than to start with Carl Woese's article
"A New Biology for a New Century," which is available on the Internet
and may be downloaded free. The full reference may be found in
the bibliography. I did not myself come across Woese's article until
the text of this book was substantially complete, so I have not been
able to pursue systematically the far-reaching implications of Woese's

work. It would be difficult to overstate the importance of Woese's own appraisal of the significance of those implications.

3. Again, the discussion at *http:www.entropylaw.com* is relevant.

4. Kevin Lynch, *What Time Is This Place?*, page 187.

5. Virtually any of the BBC documentaries made by David Attenborough, and shown on television in 2006 under the title *The Living Planet* give examples.

6. See, for example, Manfred Clynes discussing "unidirectional rate sensitivity" in *Sentics*. Langer touches on the evolution of this distinction in *Mind*, vol. 1, page 384. note. The patterns of neuronal activity involved are elucidated effectively in the entry on "Nervous system" in *The Oxford Companion to the Mind*, edited by Richard L. Gregory, published in 1987 by the Oxford University Press.

7. Nymph "soldier" aphids of the genus *Nipponaphis monzeni* die by exuding some two-thirds of their body mass in jelly-like form to repair the galls on which they live. (Kurosu, U.; Aoki, S.; and Fukatsu, T., "Self-sacrificing gall repair by aphid nymphs." *Proceedings of the Royal Society of London B (Supplement), Biology Letters*, 2003; 270: S12–S14.) Apparently the only importance to the communal entity of any individual member is whether it fulfills a necessary function. This is akin to our own case, as when our white blood cells "sacrifice" themselves similarly in guarding us against infections.

8. E. Laurence Palmer and H. Seymour Fowler discuss a number of such forms in *Fieldbook of Natural History* (2nd edition). McGraw-Hill Book Company, New York, 1975. Page 394.

9. Spiders make webs to trap their dinner; bower-birds create elaborate stage-sets to attract a mate; the brush turkeys of Australia carefully construct and tend piles of rotting vegetation to incubate their fertilized eggs. (Welty, *The Life of Birds*, page 307.) Beavers fell trees, build dams, and construct lodges. Bees build honeycombs, termites build cooperative dwellings—sometimes with rain-shedding roofs. All these examples and many others are documented with color photographs and precise diagrams in *Animal Architecture* by Karl Von Frisch. Harcourt, Brace, Jovanovich, New York and London. 1974.

10. I am overstating the case. The primary difficulty with languages in attempting to produce adequate internal representations of the physical world is that they cannot produce the vivid impact of directly

experienced events. For example, I can tell you about my experience upon jumping into the frigid November waters of Howe Sound in British Columbia a few years back, but you'd be hard put to know what that experience was really like, unless you yourself had done something similar, and had a vivid experiential memory of it. This deficiency of language is the reason for our attempting to compensate for it by the use of escalating, inflationary terms in our vocabulary. Even as we tell fish stories, I suspect, our gestures to give a picture of the size of the fish become the more extravagant as we try to represent adequately the quality of the feeling we had in the actual experience.

11. In *Theoretical Biology.*

12. I have, perhaps, fallen into the trap of thinking of those creatures with larger potential repertoires as being more developed than other organisms. All creatures alive in the world today are, however, superbly adapted to the ecological niche in which they live. In this respect, then, all creatures are on a par with one another. "Advanced" is a residue in my own consciousness of the hubris with which humankind has tended to appraise itself in relation to other living forms.

13. Edward Pols, in "The Philosophical Knowledge of the Person," terms this the "ontic power" of the organism.

14. The rest of Nature consists not simply of other creatures, of course, and the pressure that their adjustments to survive place on everything else, but also the entire balance of the physical forces that constitute the constantly changing matrix in which everything lives. James Lovelock and Lynn Margulis are probably primarily responsible for drawing our attention to this extraordinary constantly equilibrating system. Their work is persuasively presented and discussed by John Gribbin in *Deep Simplicity.* Lovelock's most recent thinking may be found in *The Vanishing Face of Gaia.* Margulis' classic overview of the issues involved may be found in *Symbiotic Planet.*

Chapter Two. Human Ambients

1. Joel Carl Welty in *The Life of Birds,* page 77 goes so far as to state "The eye of the bird has reached a state of perfection found in no other animal."

2. Perhaps Carl Sagan's book *Pale Blue Dot* gives one of the best inventories of our constantly expanding perceptual ambient.

3. David Pye, *The Nature of Design*, page 7.

4. Susanne K. Langer, in her introduction to Ernst Cassirer's *Language and Myth*, page viii.

5. Strictly speaking, "centricity" and "off-centeredness" are the terms Marjorie Grene uses in her presentation and discussion in English of the work of the German biologist-philosopher Helmuth Plessner. Grene discusses Plessner's thought, and that of Adolph Portmann, F. I. J. Buytendijk, Erwin W. Straus, and Kurt Goldstein in her *Approaches to a Philosophical Biology*.

6. Because human beings have, by virtue of our symbolizing abilities, become so much more powerful than other animals in the range of effects we can have on our surrounding world, human centric activity has larger implications for our biosphere than the centric activity of any other creature. The centricity of humanity as a species has contributed to the disregard of the very ecological balance upon which our own survival depends.

7. Susanne Langer, in *Mind*, vol. II, page 129. For a more complete comparison of animal and human sensibility, the whole of volume two of Langer's *Mind: An Essay on Human Feeling* would be difficult to match.

8. I believe the term was first used in this way by Carl Rogers, in "The Necessary and Sufficient Conditions for Therapeutic Personality Change." Its use in the psychotherapeutic literature was probably strengthened by Robert Katz's *Empathy, Its Nature and Uses*. Katz, and many psychotherapists with Rogerian leanings, were struggling to understand how to reconcile an objective appraising stance with one that conveyed to the client their deep sense of fellowship with the client's suffering. There is now a substantial literature on empathy that can be accessed through the Wikipedia entry on the Internet.

9. Otto Pollak, *Integrating Sociological and Psychoanalytic Concepts*. Russell Sage Foundation, New York. 1956.

10. A thorough exposition of the hypothesized dynamics in family life that contribute to such undifferentiation may be found in Reiner and Kaufman, *Character Disorders in Parents of Delinquents*. 1959.

11. John Donne, *Devotions Upon Emergent Occasions*. No. 17. 1624.

12. This is because a person with no true differentiation of self is likely to be in constant fear of losing the very possibility of being a self.

13. Ernst Cassirer, in *An Essay on Man* and also *The Philosophy of Symbolic Forms,* prefers "symbolic ambient," which is undoubtedly the more inclusive term. I find "conceptual ambient" easier to articulate for my purposes in this book, since I wanted to emphasize the mental processes involved in the making of representations. Cassirer took on the larger task of analyzing the historical evolution of symbolic forms, and thus the very evolution of mind.

14. The author of that hypothesis, Rupert Sheldrake, nevertheless continues to press his case. The pros and cons of his theory of "morphic resonance" are documented on the Internet.

15. It's important to recognize that intelligence shows itself in a large variety of forms—graphical, kinesthetic, musical, organizational, and instrumental—besides the more traditionally discerned verbal, mathematical, and logical forms.

16. This figure simply represents a kind of snapshot, and does not deal with the dynamic interaction between the various ambients over time.

17. Susanne Langer, *Mind,* vol. II, pages 77–78.

18. Russell Hoban, *Turtle Diary.*

Chapter Three. Belief

1. The Anthropophagi song appears in the collection "At the Drop of a Hat."

2. See, for example, Lev Semenovich Vygotsky's *Thought and Language.*

3. Reported by Lucien Price in *Dialogues of Alfred North Whitehead,* page 196.

4. What he said, in part, was "The words or the language, as they are written or spoken, do not seem to play any role in my mechanism of thought. . . . Conventional words or other signs have to be sought for *laboriously* only in a secondary stage." [my emphasis]: Einstein, *Ideas and Opinions,* pages 25–26.

   Arthur Koestler discusses this and similar statements by other scientists more fully in *The Act of Creation.*

5. A succinct account of the issues involved may be found in Simon

Baron-Cohen's article "The Short Life of a Diagnosis," in the November 10th. 2009 edition of *The New York Times.*

6. *Deaf in America,* by Carol Padden and Tom Humphries (Harvard University Press, 1988) examines the controversy in detail.

7. Paul A. Kolers, "Translation and Bilingualism," in George A. Miller, (ed.) *Communication, Language and Meaning: Psychological Perspectives.*

8. Kevin Lynch, *What Time is This Place?* page 132.

9. Different writers have proposed many other terms, all of them well-nigh synonymous with this one. In the bibliography, you'll find "schema," "meta-schema," "image," "cognitive map," "ideogram," and so on. The central idea in all is that there is an organizing internal conceptual system in the brain. I prefer "frame," since that is the term used by Langer, Cassirer, Whitehead, Wittgenstein, and Burke. Goffman's use of it concentrates rather on its constituting the kinds of interactional templates we use to determine how to behave in social roles.

10. Kenneth Burke, in *Permanence and Change,* page 101.

11. For example John Bowlby, *Attachment and Loss,* vol. I.

Chapter Four. Survival, and Opportunity

1. These are probably the most difficult to tease out, for they exist independently of verbal systems. To take graphic representations as simply one example, consider the difficulty "western" peoples have in approaching the art of China and Japan, where western conventions of perspective are displaced. We might also consider the different assumptions contained in the structure of musical composition, or the different conceptualizations of space almost necessarily resulting from reading from right to left, rather than from left to right, and so on.

   Edward Hall's book *Beyond Culture* gives many examples of differing cultural assumptions beyond those contained in verbal systems.

2. Erving Goffman, *Frame Analysis.*

3. Wittgenstein, *Philosophical Investigations,* section 114. (*Tractatus* 4–5).

4. For example, in Thomas Kuhn, *The Structure of Scientific Revolutions,* and Jerome Ravetz, *Scientific Knowledge and Its Social Problems.*

5. Wittgenstein, *Tractatus Logico Philosophicus.* "Whereof one cannot speak, thereof one must be silent." (Final proposition)
6. A. N. Whitehead, in *The Function of Reason*, page 33.
7. A. N. Whitehead, in *Adventures of Ideas.*
8. I deal with this and other such types of closed-mindedness in Chapter Nine, but it's not a bad idea to mention at this stage that many such systems contain within themselves ready-made explanations for contrary evidence, in order to justify why it should be disqualified. Senator Joe McCarthy, for example, during the hearings of the House Un-American Activities Committee in the nineteen-fifties, considered those who refused to testify before the committee de facto communists. Similarly, it was easy for some practitioners of psychoanalysis to dismiss criticisms of psychoanalytic theory as simply giving evidence of neurotic functioning on the part of the critic. (See, for example, the discussion by Matt Ridley in *Nature Via Nurture,* pages 101–105). Interestingly, Burke was vilified at the communist-dominated American Writers Congress in 1935 because he suggested in his paper "Revolutionary Symbolism in America" that "people" was a better collective term for discussing problems of inequality than the term "workers," which of course was seen as a synonym for those who were oppressed. His critics correctly saw that this would diminish the significance of the polarizing terms "oppressed" and "oppressors," which were necessary to promote the Marxist idea of "revolution" in the Party's manifesto. Burke's speech and an analysis of it by Frank Lentricchia appear in Herbert W. Simons and Trevor Melia, *The Legacy of Kenneth Burke.*
9. I. F. Stone deals with this issue at some length in *The Trial of Socrates,* pages 56–67, where he notes that Socrates' "negative dialectic" became a significant factor in his prosecution for treason. "Socrates was the master of a negative dialectic that could destroy any and every definition or proposition put to him. But he rarely offered a proposition of his own."
10. Jerome Bruner, *Towards a Theory of Instruction.*
11. Russell gives a somewhat different account of this exchange in his autobiography. Unfortunately, I have not yet been successful in tracking down my source for this particular account. Whitehead's biographer, Victor Lowe, summarized the relationship with Russell in the following way: "A wonderful thing about their collaboration

[was] the perfect preservation of the individuality of each partner, made possible by their mutual respect and affection." He also quotes from Russell's *Portraits from Memory*, pages 39–40. The quotation in essence substantiates the content and tone of the incident I've described.

12. A very moving example was made available to participants in the Eleventh International Birth Conference, held in Baltimore in 1995. They were shown a videotape of the dramatic difference between the behaviors of two groups of babies in the first few minutes of extra-uterine life. The babies who were dried, then placed on the mother's abdomen and kept warm by the heat of her body and a towel would usually begin "a crawl which ends with latching on to the mother's nipple." (Dr John Kennel). Studies in Sweden have shown that such babies succeed with breast-feeding, and will breast-feed longer than babies who were subject to more traditional hospital practices. A tape that showed babies who had been separated from their mothers for observation dramatically demonstrated that such infants, despite great efforts, were unable independently to succeed in reaching the breast. In the account I received from the CBC about this conference, it was reported that "you could hear the hearts breaking in the audience." My source is the transcript of the CBC *Ideas* broadcast of November 22, 1996 (ID 9670), available from CBC *Ideas* Transcripts, P.O. Box 500, Station A, Toronto, Ontario, M5W 1E6.

13. Some years ago, when one of my two daughters was in a parent-participation playschool, one of the other children inadvertently stumbled against a chair and knocked it over. Her mother ran over to help her up, and then encouraged her to slap at the chair, at the same time saying, "Bad chair!" Obviously, indoctrination into blaming others and thus justifying the inflicting of hurt on them can occur very early.

14. William Carlos Williams, "Of Asphodel, that greeny flower," in *Journey to Love*. Random House, New York. 1955.

15. Daniel Essertier. Quoted in English by Susanne Langer, in *Mind*, vol. III, pages 20–21.

16. Langer, *Mind*, vol. III, page 22.

17. The U.S. government's authorizing the torture of prisoners at Guantanamo Bay, and the similar policy of "rendering" prisoners to

countries in which they would be tortured, are simply the most recent examples.

18. In my local newspaper two days ago there was an item reporting Iran's proposal to enshrine in law the condemning to death of former Muslims who had renounced their religion.

Chapter Five. Error

1. I put this in quotes in order to register my uneasiness about using the word in this context. The next paragraph clarifies the reason for my doubts.

2. As, for example, in Frank T. Vertosick, Jr., *The Genius Within.* I suspect that Vertosick was unknowingly pulled in the direction of attributing that ability to the motives of particular strains by the syntactic subject/predicate structure of the English language. I recently became aware of the strength of that tug as I reviewed some of my own sentences in the earlier chapters, a notable example being the form of the sentence in which I spoke of the fig plant as if it were itself the agent in "managing to engineer its survival." I should have taken more seriously Kenneth Burke's comment that the forms of our language sometimes "think for us."

3. Abraham Kaplan, in *The Conduct of Enquiry,* page 143. Kaplan is paraphrasing T. Abel, "The Operation called 'Verstehen,'" *American Journal of Sociology* 54 (1948–49) pages 211–218.

4. The term was originally used by Clifford Geertz in "Thick Description: toward an interpretative theory of culture," in Geertz, Clifford, *The Interpretation of Cultures.* Basic Books, New York, 1973.

5. Magoroh Maruyama, in "Hierarchists, Individualists and Mutualists."

6. Charles W. Morris, *Signs, Language, and Behavior.* Prentice Hall, New York. 1946.

7. Jerome Bruner, *Towards a Theory of Instruction.*

8. Jerome Bruner, op. cit.

9. Joel Carl Welty documents and illustrates these experiments in *The Life of Birds,* pages 162–163. The original experiments are reported in N. Tinbergen, "Social releasers, and the experimental method required for their study." *Wilson Bulletin,* 60: pages 6–51.

10. Joel Carl Welty, op. cit. page 157.

11. The line is from Thomas Gray's "Elegy in a Country Churchyard."

12. See, for example, Lev Vygotsky's *Thought and Language.*

13. Evidenced, at some length, by Karl Popper, in *The Logic of Scientific Discovery,* by Abraham Kaplan in the first chapter ("Methodology") of *The Conduct of Enquiry,* and, undoubtedly, by many others also.

14. William Broad and Nicholas Wade's book gives, sadly, many examples.

15. Albert Einstein, inscription in Fine Hall, Princeton University.

16. Alfred North Whitehead, *The Function of Reason,* page 11.

17. Abraham Kaplan, *The Conduct of Enquiry,* page 28.

18. Kenneth Burke, in *Permanence and Change,* page 243.

19. Ursula Franklin, *The Real World of Technology,* page 56.

20. Robert Bringhurst, *The Beauty of the Weapons: Collected Poems, 1972–1982.* The Modern Canadian Poets. McClelland and Stewart, Toronto. 1982.

21. It's likely that most of us are only selectively attuned to these. It's particularly disturbing that the news media contribute substantially to the prevalence of such terms by failing to question—and thus implicitly accepting—the logic of the assumptions underlying them. "Ethnic cleansing" presents as one of the worst, but we also encounter "plausible deniability," "female circumcision" (as a euphemism for clitoridectomy), and a host of others. The most recently coined is, perhaps, "intelligent design." A somewhat different issue is raised by our familiarity with terms that, upon investigation, may turn out to contain moral values we would do well not to dismiss. Some of us use the word "circumcision" with little thought for its implications. Fortunately, more of us—including a significantly increasing number of medical practitioners—are aware that such a procedure constitutes a physical abuse, and thus violates the rights of the person, as stated in the Universal Declaration of Human Rights adopted by the United Nations. A corrective renaming would probably require something like "genital mutilation."

22. Kenneth Burke, *Counter Statement.* pages 140–141 et seq.

23. Possibly it's trivial to document this, but I have a fond memory of the occasion, which occurred, I believe, in 1954. The title of the lecture was something like "The Nature of Poetry," and was delivered by Dr. David Hemmings of the French department at the (then) University College of Leicester.

24. Susanne Langer pursued the implications of this distinction through-out her career, but at first, most specifically in relation to music, in *Philosophy in a New Key.* pages 204–245.
25. Kenneth Burke, *Permanence and Change,* page 257.
26. In late 2008, people of socialistic bent (and not only in the U.S.) were struck by the supreme irony of the creation of a government "rescue package" for the banks, who were themselves prime defenders of the fiction of a "free market" in the U.S.

Chapter Six. Optimizing Opportunity

1. "Lynx envers nos pareils, et taupes envers nous." Jean de la Fontaine, *Fables.* Book One, Fable Six, "La Besace." (If you can read it in French, I guarantee this fable will have you laughing out loud.)
2. Jakob Von Uexküll, *Theoretical Biology.* He conceptualized the difference as one between the number of "moment signs" that different perceivers were capable of registering in a specific time interval. Young people register more moment signs than do older people. The difference progresses with age.

Chapter Seven. Safeguarding Identity

1. Susanne Langer documents and discusses the studies upon which this statement is based in *Mind, An Essay on Human Feeling,* vol. II, pages 113–116.
2. Paul McClean, *A Triune Concept of the Brain and Behavior.*
3. Alexander Lowen, *The Language of the Body.*
4. Ekman and Friesen, "Non-verbal Leakage and Clues to Deception."
5. Jon Elster, "Belief, Bias, and Ideology." Kenneth Burke comments similarly that "the mere fact that something is to a man's interests is no guarantee that he will be interested in it." (*Permanence and Change,* page 38.)
6. D. M. McKay, "Formal Analysis of Communicative Processes."
7. The concert pianist Leon Fleischer has spoken movingly of his experience of losing the use of his left hand in the accompanying notes to his CD recital "Two Hands." (Vanguard Classics ATM CD 1551.)

8. See, for example, Antonio R. Damasio, *Descartes' Error,* pages 100–108.

9. The Westray Mine Public Enquiry Executive Summary, *The Westray Story: A Predictable Path to Disaster,* is a moving inventory of such maneuvers. At the time of writing, this report was still available on the Internet. News reports of the mine disasters in Shanxi province in China in early 2010 gave evidence of similar patterns of disregard.

10. Stephen Hawking reports on this, wryly, in the movie version of *A Brief History of Time.*

11. Ivan Boszormenyi-Nagy very effectively diagrams some of these patterns of interaction in *Intensive Family Therapy.*

12. Claude Steiner, *Scripts People Live.*

13. Oliver Sacks, in *Awakenings,* page 25, is uncompromising in his appraisal: "Rigorous institutions are . . . coercive, being, in effect, *external neuroses.*" [The emphasis is his]. Sacks was discussing mental institutions, but it's not unreasonable to extend his analogy to social structures which less obviously contribute to the maintenance of unhealthy human interactions.

14. Erving Goffman, in *Frame Analysis,* gives many examples.

Chapter Eight. Cooperation

1. Although marriages are not, strictly speaking, affiliative, they also may show, over time, similar changes of dynamic, and for very similar reasons.

2. Bureaucratization, Kenneth Burke reminds us, is not simply a feature of organizational structures, but also of modes of thought and interaction in other circumstances. He called this "the bureaucratization of the imaginative," in *Attitudes Towards History,* pages 225–229.

3. This was particularly apparent in the course of the Industrial Revolution.

4. The story is told of Lao Tse, on the verge of leaving his very formal society in disgust, being persuaded to set down his thoughts. In consequence, he wrote the *Tao Te Ching.* The authorship we attribute to him, of course, but for the motivation we should also thank the unknowns whose efforts were rewarded. Individuals make a difference.

5. A similarly devastating example is thoroughly documented by John Stalker in his book *The Stalker Affair* (Viking Books, New York, 1978). Stalker had been called upon to investigate the role of the Royal Ulster Constabulary in the shooting deaths of six suspected Irish Republican Army members in separate incidents in Ireland in 1982. He was about to recommend the criminal prosecution of the suspected killers when he was suspended from the enquiry following allegations of criminal activity. He was only able to clear his name by going to court at his own expense. He was vindicated, but nevertheless not reinstated, and the subsequent replacement report was never made available to the public. A subsequent coroner's report concluded without a decision, as the government refused to authorize release of Stalker's findings, or the evidence upon which he had based them. As I write (it is now 2010) Wikipedia reports that members of the victims' families are still attempting to achieve open inquest hearings for the victims.

Chapter Nine. Change

1. Lilian Ripple, Ernestina Alexander, and Bernice Polemis, in *Motivation, Capacity and Opportunity: Studies in Casework Theory and Practice.* Also, Sarah B. Wright, in *The Client's Confidence of Success.* The findings of this series of studies are of enormous importance, and their implications are significant far beyond the arena of social casework practice.
2. This was declared by the character Pogo, in the comic strip of that name, in 1970. Pogo's inventor was Walt Kelly, who died in 1973. The history of the Pogo cartoon is fascinating, and nicely documented on the Internet.
3. An unfortunate problem associated with the making of distinctions (necessary, of course, for any kind of thinking whatsoever) is that they lead us easily into polarities, and this is poignantly apparent in Walt Kelly's attempt to transcend them by showing that we are, in a sense, at war with ourselves. The very simile of war, then, since it requires (almost by definition) a winner and a loser, is inadequate and indeed downright misleading as we try to come to grips with a unified conception of ourselves in which no aspect of ourselves need be excluded. Our very society is riven with the acceptance of polarity

as an unavoidable aspect of the human condition. Its presence is institutionalized in our legal, political, and economic systems. Undoubtedly, there are many examples of my own struggle to deal with this throughout this book, and not simply in this chapter, where it is inevitably the major focus of my attention. A significant attempt to deal with the issue head-on was made by Kenneth Boulding, in *A Primer on Social Dynamics*.

4. I wonder if this kind of polarizing tendency is more pervasive in societies with a more conscious awareness of their own revolutionary history? The remark is attributed to Baudelaire, and was presumably made in conversation. ("Il faut épater le bourgeois.")

5. George Bernard Shaw, who was nevertheless ambivalent about it. (See a little later in the text.) Shaw's extended preface to *Back to Methusalah* discusses the implications of the aphorism at some length.

6. Kenneth Burke, *Counter Statement*, page 119.

7. George Orwell may have been right, but the actual situation was a bit more complicated than that. Shaw's compulsion to write extended prefaces to the plays was likely motivated by his awareness that the "shock" doctrine incorporated in the dramas themselves would in itself be insufficiently persuasive. One can imagine engaging in dialogue with Shaw around issues raised in the prefaces, but the plays themselves scarcely evoke a desire to do likewise. Drama is rarely an invitation to dialogue—a characteristic of which Shaw was acutely aware.

8. Northrop Frye, *Words With Power*, page 17.

9. Ibid., page 15.

10. Ibid., page 18.

11. One could derive a rich inventory of polarizing accusations, including arguments ad hominem, from virtually any election campaign. Our most recent experience of this in North America at the time of writing is the presidential election of 2008 in the U.S.

12. Northrop Frye, *Words With Power*, page 16.

13. This is attributed by Burke (in *A Rhetoric of Motives*, page 79) to the first or third century CE writer known as Longinus; in *On the Sublime*, he defines this as the aim of poetry.

14. Percy Bysshe Shelley, *A Defence of Poetry*. 1821.

15. Actor Simon Callow discusses Brecht's concept "Verfremdungseffekt" at some length in his book *Charles Laughton: A Difficult Actor*

(page 167). Apparently, that word was Brecht's approximation in German of Shklovsky's Russian neologism "ostraniene." (See following note.)

16. Viktor Shklovsky coined the term "ostraniene" in his *Theory of Prose*. Benjamin Sher, his translator, discusses the problem of translating this neologism into a readily understandable English equivalent in his introduction to the English version of the book. In order to keep the unexpectedness, but also the precision of the Russian word, Sher opted for "enstrangement" in English. It's obviously not possible to pursue all the ramifications of this idea here, but to implement it as a principle guiding attempts to produce change is no easy matter, since we ourselves may first need to overcome our own bits of blindness in order to promote the best kinds of circumstances for others to encounter theirs.

    Two rather different anecdotes suggest the importance of other factors in permitting enstrangement to have an effect. In the first, Canadian artist Toni Onley, visiting the Canadian Arctic aboard an icebreaker in order to paint the ice- and seascapes of the far North, encountered some interesting reactions to his pictures by the crew. Members of the ship's crew were of course very familiar with the ice-laden seas. None claimed to be able to see the subtle colors of Onley's pictures in the natural world around them. Mauves, blues, pinks, and variations of other colors eluded them. "But it's all white up here!" one of them protested. Onley suggested they turn their heads upside-down when looking at the ice- and seascapes, and they would be able to see the colors he had seen. All of them did. (The event was documented in the KCTS documentary film of Onley's trip.)

    The second anecdote is a fictional one. In the Peter Weir movie *Dead Poets' Society*, the English teacher, portrayed by Robin Williams, was able to dramatize the effect of different perspectives to his students by having them, in turn, survey their classroom from the perspective allowed by standing upright on top of his desk. The results were mixed; some of the students were clearly unable to allow themselves to savor the experience.

17. I suggested in my introduction that attempting to see ourselves as if from the outside was a helpful guiding suggestion for any strategy that would have the promise of unlocking us from centric preoccupations. It's probably apparent, then, that this paragraph is particularly

significant in portraying a major difficulty facing humankind. In short, if we consider the protagonist as humankind itself, then we may need to find some quite dramatic way to better represent ourselves to ourselves if any major shift of sensibility is to be achieved. Events in recent years have illustrated this in what to most of us was probably a completely unexpected way. First, we had the perspective-altering experience of seeing our planet itself from the outside—"the big blue marble"—and then subsequently seeing our planet in its cosmological neighborhood, with Voyager's photograph of the "pale blue dot" of Earth as it was just about to disappear from the range of Voyager's cameras. Carl Sagan eloquently discusses the implications of this shifted point-of-view in his book. I take these events as seriously as I can in the next chapter.

18. Paulo Freire, *Pedagogy of the Oppressed.* Unfortunately, although Freire's "program" might at first seem to transcend the limitations of his fundamentally Marxist stance to social change, he cannot seem to rid himself of the conviction that change depends more on the awareness of the oppressed than on that of the oppressors. (These polarizing terms are, of course, stubbornly Marxist, and recall the difficulties that Kenneth Burke faced in 1935, when he was trying to help the writers at the American Writers Congress transcend them.) See also note number 8, in Chapter Four above.

Chapter Ten. A Better Question—and an Answer

1. Albert Camus' novel is still available in English, with the title translated as *The Stranger,* or *The Outsider.*

2. A most moving expression of this aspiration was reported by Oliver Sacks, in his account of meeting with Temple Grandin, the autistic person who is featured in the essay "An Anthropologist on Mars," which appears in Sacks' book of that title. Dr. Grandin's statement is to be found on page 296. The complete essay is a very powerful documentation of the force of that aspiration in the life of a truly remarkable individual.

3. Paul Feyerabend, in *Against Method.* Feyerabend was being playfully provocative; the book is not against method, but against any too-exclusive definition of it.

Bibliography

Adler, Alfred. *Understanding Human Nature.* A Fawcett Premier Book, Fawcett World Library, New York. 1968.

Arendt, Hannah. *On Violence.* Harcourt, Brace, and World, New York. 1969.

Argyle, Michael. *Social Interaction.* Methuen and Co., London. 1969.

Atkins, Peter. *Galileo's Finger: The Ten Great Ideas of Science.* Oxford University Press, Oxford. 2003.

Barrett, Cyril (ed.). *Wittgenstein: Lectures and Conversations on Aesthetics, Psychology and Religious Belief.* University of California Press, Berkeley. N.d.

Barrett, William. *Irrational Man: A Study in Existential Philosophy.* Anchor Books, Doubleday, New York. 1958.

———. *The Illusion of Technique: A Search for Meaning in a Technological Civilization.* Anchor Books, Doubleday, Garden City, New York. 1979.

Barrett-Lennard, G. T. "Dimensions of Therapist Response as Causal Factors in Therapeutic Change." In *Psychological Monographs.* 76: no. 43. 1962.

Barzun, Jacques. *The House Of Intellect.* Harper Torchbooks, Harper and Row, New York. 1961.

Bertalanffy, Ludwig Von. *General System Theory.* George Braziller, New York. 1968.

———. "The Tree of Knowledge." In Kepes, Gyorgy, (ed.), *Sign, Signal, and Image.* Studio Vista, George Braziller, London. 1966.

Bieri, James; Atkins, A. L.; Briar, S.; Leaman, R. L.; Miller, H.; and Tripodi, T. *Clinical and Social Judgment: The Discrimination of Behavioral Information.* John Wiley and Sons, New York. 1966.

Bloom, Allen. *The Closing of the American Mind.* Touchstone, Simon and Schuster, Inc., New York. 1987.

Bloor, David. *Knowledge and Social Imagery.* Routledge and Kegan Paul, London. 1976.

Blumer, Herbert. *Symbolic Interactionism: Perspective and Method.* Prentice-Hall, New Jersey. 1969.

Boszormenyi-Nagy, Ivan, and Framo, James L. (eds.). *Intensive Family Therapy: Theoretical and Practical Aspects.* Hoeber Medical Division, Harper and Row Publishers, New York. 1965.

Boulding, Kenneth. *A Primer on Social Dynamics.* The Free Press, New York. 1970.

———. *The Image: Knowledge in Life and Society.* Ann Arbour, University of Michigan Press. 1956.

Bowlby, John. *Attachment and Loss.* (Vol. 1: *Attachment.*) (2nd edition.) Basic Books, New York. 1999. (Originally published 1969.)

———. *Attachment and Loss.* (Vol. 2: *Separation: Anxiety and Anger.*) Hogarth Press, London. 1973.

———. *Attachment and Loss.* (Vol. 3: *Loss, Sadness and Depression.*) Hogarth Press, London. 1980.

Briffault, Robert. *Psyche's Lamp: A Re-evaluation of Psychological Principles as Foundation of All Thought.* George Allen and Unwin, London. 1921.

Broad, William, and Wade, Nicholas. *Betrayers of the Truth.* Simon and Schuster, New York. 1982.

Bronowsky, Jacob. *The Identity of Man.* The Natural History Press, Garden City, New York. 1966.

Bruner, Jerome S. *Towards a Theory of Instruction.* The Belknap Press of Harvard University Press, Cambridge, Massachusetts, and London, England. 1966.

———. and Postman, L. "Perception, Cognition, and Behavior." In *Journal of Personality,* 18: 14–31. 1949.

Burke, Kenneth. *Attitudes Towards History.* (3rd revised edition.) University of California Press, Berkeley. 1984.

———. *Counter-Statement.* Paperback, University of California Press, Berkeley. 1968. (Originally published, Harcourt, Brace, New York. 1931.)

———. *A Grammar of Motives.* (2nd edition.) University of California Press, Berkeley. 1969.

———. *Language as Symbolic Action: Essays on Life, Literature, and Method.* University of California Press, Berkeley. 1966.

———. *Permanence and Change: An Anatomy of Purpose.* (3rd revised edition.) University of California Press, Berkeley. 1984.

———. *The Philosophy of Literary Form: Studies in Symbolic Action.* (3rd revised edition.) University of California Press, Berkeley. 1973.

———. *A Rhetoric of Motives.* (2nd edition.) University of California Press, Berkeley. 1969.

———. *The Rhetoric of Religion: Studies in Logology.* University of California Press, Berkeley. 1970.

Carpenter, Edmund. *"Oh, What a Blow That Phantom Gave Me!".* Holt, Rinehart and Winston, New York. 1973.

Cassirer, Ernst. *An Essay on Man: An Introduction to the Philosophy of Human Culture.* Yale University Press, New Haven and London. 1972. (Originally published 1944.)

———. *Language and Myth.* Translated by Susanne K. Langer. Harper and Bros., New York and London. 1946. (Originally published in German, 1926.)

———. *The Philosophy of Symbolic Forms.* Yale University Press, New Haven and London. Vol. 1 and vol. 2, 1955. Vol. 3, 1957.

Childe, V. Gordon. *Society and Knowledge.* George Allen and Unwin Ltd., London. 1956.

Clynes, Manfred. *Sentics: The Touch of Emotions.* Anchor Press, Doubleday, Garden City, New York. 1977.

Cohen, Morris R. and Nagel, Ernest. *An Introduction to Logic and Scientific Method.* Harcourt, Brace and World, Inc., New York. 1934.

Crick, F. S. C. "Thinking About the Brain." In *Scientific American,* vol. 241, no. 3:219–232.

Colodny, Robert G. (ed.). *Beyond the Edge of Certainty.* Prentice-Hall Inc., Englewood Cliffs, New Jersey. 1965.

Damasio, Antonio R. *Descartes' Error: Emotion, Reason, and the Human Brain.* G. P. Putnam's Sons, New York. 1994.

Darwin, Charles. *The Expression of Emotion in Man and Animals.* Phoenix Books, The University of Chicago Press, Chicago and London. 1965. (Originally published 1872.)

Dawkins, Richard. *Climbing Mount Improbable.* Bantam Books. 1996.

———. *The Ancestor's Tale: A Pilgrimage to the Dawn of Evolution.* Weidenfeld and Nicolson, London. 2004.

———. *The God Delusion.* Bantam Press. 2006.

Dennett, Daniel C. *Darwin's Dangerous Idea: Evolution and the Meanings of Life.* Simon and Schuster Paperbacks, New York. 1995.

Diamond, Jared M. *Collapse: How Societies Choose to Fail or Succeed.* Viking Press, New York. 2005.

Ehrlich, Paul R. *Human Natures: Genes, Cultures, and the Human Prospect.* A Shearwater Book, Island Press, Washington, D.C. 2000.

Einstein, Albert. *Ideas and Opinions.* Wings Books, New York/Avenel, New Jersey. 1954.

Ekman, Paul, and Friesen, Wallace W. "Non-Verbal Leakage and Clues to Deception." In Argyle, Michael (ed.). *Social Encounters.* Methuen and Co., London. 1969.

Elster, Jon. "Belief, Bias, and Ideology." In Hollis and Lukes (eds.), *Rationality and Relativism.* Basil Blackwell, Oxford. 1982.

Empson, William. *Some Versions of Pastoral.* The Hogarth Press, London. 1986. (Originally published 1935.)

Essertier, Daniel. *Les Formes Inférieures de l'Explication.* Alcan, Paris. 1927.

Feyerabend, Paul K. *Against Method: Outline of an Anarchical Theory of Knowledge.* Humanities Press. 1975.

———. "Problems of Empiricism." In Colodney, Robert G. (ed.), *Beyond the Edge of Certainty.* Prentice-Hall, Inc., Englewood Cliffs, New Jersey. 1965.

Fogelin, Robert. *Walking the Tightrope of Reason: The Precarious Life of a Rational Animal.* Oxford University Press. Oxford. 2003.

Frank, P. (ed.) *The Validation of Scientific Theories.* The Beacon Press, Boston. 1954.

Franklin, Ursula. *The Real World of Technology.* CBC Enterprises, Toronto, Canada. 1990.

Freire, Paulo. *Pedagogy of the Oppressed.* Herder and Herder, New York. 1970.

Frye, Northrop. *Anatomy of Criticism: Four Essays.* Princeton University Press, Princeton, New Jersey. 1990. (Originally published 1957.)

———. *The Great Code: The Bible and Literature.* Penguin Books. 1990. (Originally published 1983.)

———. *Words with Power: Being a Second Study of The Bible and Literature.* Penguin Books. 1992. (Originally published 1990.)

Galbraith, J. K. *The Anatomy of Power.* Houghton, Mifflin Company, Boston. 1983.

Geschwind, Norman. "The Brain and Language." In Miller, George A. (ed.). *Communication, Language and Meaning.* Basic Books, New York. 1973.

Ghiselin, Brewster (ed.). *The Creative Process: A Symposium.* University of California Press, Berkeley. 1952.

Goffman, Erving. *Frame Analysis: An Essay on the Organization of Experience.* Harvard University Press, Cambridge, Massachusetts. 1974.

———. *Strategic Interaction.* Conduct and Communication Monograph 1. University of Pennsylvania Press, Philadelphia. 1969.

Gombrich, E. H. *Art and Illusion.* (2nd edition, 11th printing, with a new preface.) Princeton University Press, Princeton, New Jersey. 2000. (Originally published 1960.)

———. *The Sense of Order: A Study in the Psychology of Decorative Art.* (2nd edition) Cornell University Press, Ithaca, New York. 1984. (Originally published 1979.)

Gordon, George N. *Languages of Communication.* Hastings House, New York. 1969.

Gregory, R. L. *Eye and Brain: The Psychology of Seeing.* Weidenfeld and Nicolson, London. 1977. (Originally published 1966.)

———. *The Intelligent Eye.* McGraw-Hill Book Company, New York. 1970.

Grene, Marjorie. *Approaches to a Philosophical Biology.* Basic Books, New York. 1965.

———. *The Anatomy of Knowledge,* Routledge and Kegan Paul, London. 1969.

Gribbin, John. *Deep Simplicity: Bringing Order to Chaos and Complexity.* Random House, New York. 2005.

Hacking, Ian. "Language, Truth and Reason." In Hollis and Lukes (eds.), *Rationality and Relativism.* Basil Blackwell, Oxford. 1982.

Hall, Edward T. *The Silent Language.* Anchor Books, Doubleday and Co., Inc. New York. 1959.

———. *The Hidden Dimension.* Anchor Books, Doubleday and Company, Inc. New York. 1966.

———. *Beyond Culture.* Anchor Books, Doubleday and Company, Inc. New York. 1977. (Originally published 1976.)

Hanson, Norwood Russell. *Patterns of Discovery: An Enquiry into the Conceptual Foundations of Science.* Cambridge University Press, Cambridge. 1961.

Hartmann, Heinz. *Psychology and Moral Values.* International Universities Press, Inc., New York. 1960.

Hayakawa, S. I. *Language in Thought and Action.* (3rd edition.) Harcourt Brace Jovanovich Inc. New York. 1972. (Originally published 1939.)

Hinde, Robert A. (ed.). *Non-Verbal Communication.* Cambridge, at the University Press. 1972.

Hoban, Russell. *Turtle Diary.* Picador Books, London. 1975.

Hollis, Martin, and Lukes, Steven (eds.). *Rationality and Relativism.* Basil Blackwell, Oxford. 1982.

Honderich, Ted (ed.). *The Oxford Companion to Philosophy.* Oxford University Press, Oxford. 1995.

Huizenga, Johan. *Homo Ludens.* Paladin, London. 1970. (Originally published 1938.)

Illich, Ivan. *Tools for Conviviality.* Perennial Library, Harper and Row Publishers. New York. 1973.

Kaplan, Abraham. *The Conduct of Enquiry: Methodology for Behavioral Science.* Chandler Publishing Company, San Francisco. 1964.

Katz, Robert L. *Empathy: Its Nature and Uses.* The Free Press, New York. 1963.

Kepes, Gyorgy (ed.). *Sign, Symbol, and Image.* Studio Vista. George Braziller, Inc., London. 1966.

Kleinman, Arthur. *Patients and Healers in the Context of Culture: An Exploration of the Borderland between Anthropology, Medicine, and Psychiatry.* University of California Press, Berkeley. 1980.

Koestler, Arthur. *The Act of Creation.* (Revised Danube edition.) Pan Books Ltd., London. 1970.

———. *The Ghost in the Machine.* The MacMillan Company, New York. 1967.

Kohler, Wolfgang. "Direction of Processes in Living Systems." In Frank, P., (ed.). *The Validation of Scientific Theories.* Beacon Press, Boston. 1954.

Kraus, Elizabeth M. *The Metaphysics of Experience: A Companion to Whitehead's Process and Reality.* Fordham University Press, New York. 1979.

Kuhn, Thomas S. *The Structure of Scientific Revolutions.* (2nd edition, enlarged.) University of Chicago Press, Chicago. 1970. (Originally published 1962.)

Laing, Ronald D., et al. *Interpersonal Perception: A Theory and Method of Research.* Tavistock Publications, London. 1966.

Lakatos, Imre, and Feyerabend, Paul. *For and Against Method.* Edited and with an introduction by Matteo Motterlini. Chicago University Press, Chicago. 1999.

Langer, Susanne K. *Feeling and Form.* Charles Scribner and Sons, New York. 1953.

——. *Mind: An Essay on Human Feeling.* John Hopkins University Press, Baltimore and London. Vol. 1, 1967. Vol. 2, 1972. Vol. 3, 1982.

——. *Philosophy in a New Key: A Study in the Symbolism of Reason, Rite, and Art.* (3rd edition.) Harvard University Press, Cambridge, Massachusetts. 1978. (Originally published 1942.)

Levin, Samuel R. *Metaphoric Worlds: Conceptions of a Romantic Nature.* Yale University Press, New Haven and London. 1988.

Levitin, Daniel J. *This is Your Brain on Music: The Science of a Human Obsession.* Penguin Books. 2007.

——. *The World in Six Songs: How the Musical Brain Created Human Nature.* The Penguin Group, Canada. 2007.

Lovelock, James. *Homage to Gaia: The Life of an Independent Scientist.* Oxford University Press, Oxford. 2000.

——. *The Vanishing Face of Gaia: A Final Warning.* Allen Lane, an imprint of Penguin Books, London. 2009.

Lowen, Alexander. *The Language of the Body.* Collier Macmillan, New York, 1971. (Originally published by Grune and Stratton, Inc. as *The Physical Dynamics of Character Structure.* 1958.)

Luria, A. R. *Basic Problems of Neurolinguistics.* Mouton and Company, B.U., The Hague. 1976.

Lynch, Kevin. *What Time is this Place?* M.I.T. Press. 1972.

MacClean, Paul D. *A Triune Concept of the Brain and Behavior.* University of Toronto Press, Toronto. 1973.

MacKay, D. M. "Formal Analysis of Communicative Processes." In Hinde, Robert A. (ed.), *Non-Verbal Communication.* Cambridge University Press. 1972.

Margulis, Lynn. *Symbiotic Planet: A New Look at Evolution.* Phoenix Press, London. 1998.

Maruyama, Magoroh. "Hierarchists, Individualists and Mutualists: Three Paradigms among Planners." In *Futures* (April, 1974) 103–113.

———. "Epistemology of Social Science Research." in *Dialectica*, vol. 23: 229–280. 1969.

Maslow, Abraham. *The Farther Reaches of Human Nature.* The Viking Press, New York. 1971.

Masson, Jeffrey Moussaieff. *The Assault on Truth: Freud's Suppression of the Seduction Theory.* Farrar, Strauss and Giroux. 1984.

Mead, George Herbert. *Mind, Self, and Society—From the Standpoint of a Social Behaviorist.* Edited and with an introduction by Charles W. Morris. University of Chicago Press, Chicago and London. 1962. (Originally published 1934.)

Miller, George A. (ed.). *Communication, Language, and Meaning: Psychological Perspectives.* Basic Books, Inc., New York. 1973.

Monod, Jacques. *Chance and Necessity: An Essay on the Natural Philosophy of Modern Biology.* Translated by Austryn Wainhouse. Alfred A. Knopf, New York. 1971.

Montagu, Ashley. *Touching: The Human Significance of the Skin.* Harper and Row, New York. 1978. (Originally published 1971.)

Moss, Gordon E. *Illness, Immunity, and Social Interaction: The Dynamics of Bio-Social Resonation.* John Wiley and Sons, New York. 1973.

Neisser, Ulric. *Cognition and Reality.* W. H. Freeman and Company, San Francisco. 1976.

Northrop, F. S. C. *The Logic of the Sciences and the Humanities.* Meridian Books, Inc., New York. 1947. (Reprinted in 1983 by Oxbow Press.)

Ogden, C. K., and Richards, I. A. *The Meaning of Meaning.* Harcourt, Brace and World. 1946.

Ortony, Andrew (ed.). *Metaphor and Thought.* Cambridge University Press, Cambridge and New York. 1979.

Orwell, George. *Selected Essays.* Penguin Books in association with Secker and Warburg, Harmondsworth, Middlesex. 1957.

Osgood, C. E.; Suci, George J.; and Tannenbaum, Percy H. *The Measurement of Meaning.* University of Illinois Press, Urbana, Chicago and London. 1967.

Penrose, Roger. *The Emperor's New Mind.* Oxford University Press, Oxford. 1989.

Piaget, Jean. *The Origins of Intelligence in Children.* W. W. Norton and Company, New York. 1952.

Pinker, Steven. *The Stuff of Thought: Language as a Window into Human Nature.* Penguin Books. 2008.

Polanyi, Michael, and Prosch, Harry. *Meaning.* The University of Chicago Press, Chicago and London. 1975.

Polanyi, Michael. *Personal Knowledge: Towards a Post-Critical Philosophy.* (Corrected edition.) University of Chicago Press, Chicago. 1962. (Originally published 1958.)

Pols, Edward. "Philosophical Knowledge of the Person." In Marjorie Grene (ed.) *The Anatomy of Knowledge.* Routledge and Kegan Paul, London. 1969.

Popper, Karl R. *The Logic of Scientific Discovery.* Harper Torchbooks, Harper and Row, Publishers, New York. 1965. (Originally published 1959.)

———. *The Open Society and Its Enemies.* Princeton University Press, Princeton, New Jersey. Vol. 1 (5th edition), 1966. Vol. 2 (5th edition), 1966.

Price, Lucien. *Dialogues of Alfred North Whitehead.* A Mentor Book, The New American Library of World Literature, Inc., New York. 1956. (Originally published 1954.)

Pulasky, Mary Ann Spencer. *Understanding Piaget.* Harper and Row, New York. 1980.

Pye, David. *The Nature of Design.* Studio Vista, London, and Reinhold Publishing Corporation, New York. 1964.

———. *The Nature and Aesthetics of Design.* Barrie and Jenkins, London, 1978.

———. *The Nature and Art of Workmanship.* Studio Vista, London. 1971.

Rashevsky, N. "Is the Concept of the Organism as a Machine a Useful One?" In Frank, P. (ed.) *The Validation of Scientific Theories.* The Beacon Press, Boston. 1954.

Ravetz, Jerome. *Scientific Knowledge and Its Social Problems.* Oxford University Press, Oxford. 1979.

Reiner, Beatrix Simcox, and Kaufman, Irving. *Character Disorders in Parents of Delinquents.* Family Service Association of America, New York. 1959.

Ridley, Matt. *Genome: The Autobiography of a Species in 23 Chapters.* HarperCollins Publishers, New York. 2000.

———. *Nature Via Nurture: Genes, Experience, and What Makes Us Human.* HarperCollins, Toronto. 2003.

Ripple, Lilian; Alexander, Ernestine; and Polemis, Bernice W. *Motivation, Capacity, and Opportunity: Studies in Casework Theory and Practice.* Social Service Monographs. (2nd series, no. 3.) The School of Social Service Administration, The University of Chicago, Chicago. 1964.

Rogers, Carl R. "The Necessary and Sufficient Conditions of Therapeutic Personality Change." In *The Journal of Consulting Psychology,* 21: 95–103. 1957.

Rokeach, Milton. *The Open and the Closed Mind: Investigations into the Nature of Belief Systems and Personality Systems.* Basic Books, New York. 1960.

Sacks, Oliver. *Awakenings.* Vintage Books, Random House, New York. 1999. (Originally published 1990.)

———. *An Anthropologist on Mars: Seven Paradoxical Tales.* Vintage Books, Random House, New York. 1996.

———. *Musicophilia: Tales of Music and the Brain.* Random House, New York. 2007.

Sagan, Carl. *Pale Blue Dot: A Vision of The Human Future in Space.* Random House, New York. 1994.

Schachtel, Ernest G. *Metamorphosis.* Basic Books, Inc. New York. 1986.

Shklovsky, Viktor. *Theory of Prose.* Translated by Benjamin Sher. Dalkey Archive Press, Elmwood Park, Illinois. 1990. (Originally published in Russian, 1925.)

Simons, Herbert W., and Melia, Trevor. *The Legacy of Kenneth Burke.* The University of Wisconsin Press, Madison, Wisconsin. 1989.

Spitz, René. *The First Year of Life: A Psychoanalytic Study of Normal and Deviant Development in Object Relations.* International Universities Press, New York. 1965.

Stanton, Alfred H., and Schwarz, Morris S. *The Mental Hospital.* Basic Books, Inc. New York. 1954.

Steiner, Claude. *Scripts People Live: Transactional Analysis of Life Scripts.* Grove Press, New York. 1974.

Steiner, George. *After Babel: Aspects of Language and Translation.* (2nd edition.) Oxford University Press, Oxford. 1992. (Originally published 1975.)

———. *In Bluebeard's Castle: Some Notes Towards the Redefinition of Culture.* Yale University Press, New Haven. 1971.

Stewart, Matthew. *The Courtier and the Heretic.* Yale University Press, New Haven. 2007.

Stone, I. F. *The Trial of Socrates.* Anchor Books, Doubleday, New York. 1989.

Storr, Anthony. *Music and the Mind.* Ballantine Books, Random House Inc., New York. 1993.

Thorpe, W. H. *Science, Man, and Morals.* Methuen and Co. Ltd., London. 1965.

Towle, Charlotte. *The Learner in Education for the Professions.* University of Chicago Press, Chicago. 1954.

Uexküll, Jakob Von. *Theoretical Biology.* Harcourt, Brace and Co., New York. 1926.

Vertosick, Frank T., Jr. *The Genius Within: Discovering the Intelligence of Every Living Thing.* Harcourt, Inc., New York, San Diego, London. 2002.

Vygotsky, Lev Semonovich. *Thought and Language.* Edited and translated by Eugenia Haufman and Gertrude Vaker. The M.I.T. Press, Cambridge, Massachusetts. 1962. (Originally published in Russian, 1934.)

Watzlawick, Paul; Weakland, John; and Fisch, Richard. *Change: Principles of Problem Formation and Problem Resolution.* W. W. Norton and Co. Inc., New York. 1974.

Watzlawick, Paul; Beavin, Janet; and Jackson, D. *Pragmatics of Human Communication: A Study in Interactional Patterns, Pathologies, and Paradoxes.* W. W. Norton and Co., Inc., New York. 1967.

Whitehead, Alfred North. *Adventures of Ideas.* The Free Press, New York. 1967. (Originally published 1933.)

———. *The Function of Reason.* Beacon Press Paperback, Boston. 1958. (Originally published 1929.)

———. *Modes of Thought.* The Free Press, Macmillan Publishing Co. Inc., New York. 1968. (Originally published 1938.)

———. *Symbolism: Its Meaning and Effect.* Fordham University Press, New York. 1985. (Originally published 1927.)

———. *Process and Reality.* (Corrected edition.) Edited by David Ray Griffin and Donald W. Sherburne. The Free Press, A Division of Macmillan Publishing Co., Inc., New York. 1978. (Originally published 1929.)

Wiener, Norbert. *The Human Use of Human Beings: Cybernetics and Society.* Avon Books, The Hearst Corporation, New York. 1970. (Originally published 1950.)

Wilding, Paul. *Professional Power and Social Welfare.* Routledge and Kegan Paul, London. 1982.

Winter, Ruth. *The Smell Book.* J. B. Lippincott Company, Philadelphia and New York. 1976.

Wittgenstein, Ludwig. *Lectures and Conversations: on Aesthetics, Psychology and Religious Belief.* Edited by Cyril Barrett from notes compiled by Yorick Smythies, Rush Rees, and James Taylor. University of California Press, Berkeley and Los Angeles. N.d. (Originally published 1938.)

——. *Notebooks 1914–1916.* (2nd edition.) Edited by G. H. von Wright and G. E. M. Anscombe. University of Chicago Press, Chicago. 1979. (Originally published 1961.)

——. *Philosophical Investigations.* (3rd edition.) Translated by G. E. M. Anscombe. Macmillan Publishing Company Inc. 1968. (Originally published 1953.)

——. *Tractatus Logico-Philosophicus.* Translated and prepared by C. K. Ogden, with assistance from G. E. Moore, F. P. Ramsey, and Ludwig Wittgenstein. Routledge and Kegan Paul, London. 1922. (Dover Books reprint, 1999.)

Woese, Carl R. "A New Biology for a New Century." In *Microbiology and Molecular Biology Reviews.* Vol. 68, no. 2: 173–186. American Society for Microbiology. June 2004.

Wolfe, Tom. *Radical Chic and Mau-Mauing The Flak-catchers.* Farrar, Straus, and Giroux, New York. 1970.

Wright, Sara B. *"The Client's Confidence of Success: A Factor in Casework Treatment."* Ph.D. thesis, School of Social Service Administration, University of Chicago. 1963.

Acknowledgments

MANY PEOPLE HAVE contributed to the existence of this book and the ideas it contains—some unknowingly, others in full and knowing commitment. It is impossible to give full credit where it may be due, but this is my attempt.

Primarily, my brother and I were fortunate in having parents who could envisage the possibility of a better world, and who therefore supported us in our aspirations, however different they undoubtedly were from those of many of our close contemporaries. We were also fortunate in benefiting from the opportunities opened up for us in post–World War Two Britain. It was still rare in early nineteen-fifties Britain for children of working-class parents to be able to obtain a university education, as my brother and I did.

My debt to my various mentors is also great: to L. C. Sykes at the then University College of Leicester, to Lulie Shaw at the University of Bristol, to Mary Richardson at the East London Family Service Unit, and to Elizabeth Butler, Charlotte Towle, Helen Harris Perlman, Bernece Simon, Lilian Ripple and Bernice Polemis at the School of Social Service Administration, the University of Chicago.

I cannot individually thank those who, over the years, shared with me their struggles to confront honestly their dilemmas in living. I can, however, express gratitude to them collectively for their having played a significant part in my learning to encounter my own.

It is also scarcely possible to credit in detail those who affected my thinking while I was teaching at the University of British Columbia. The students and field-instructors with whom I worked are too numerous to name, but their combined contribution was a significant one. My debt to faculty colleagues is very great: most significantly to Bill Nichols, Ben Chud, Glenda Gentleman, and George Hougham; their engagement with me still defines for me the true nature of colleagueship.

Specifically in relation to this book, I owe thanks to many: to Anne Campbell, for early encouragement, searching questions, and great practical help; to a large group of very different readers, many of whom made transformative comments: Liz Meharg, Andrée Scott, Gary Prideaux, Pam Asquith, Kees Groot, John Dowd, Beatrice Dowd, Sarah and Wendy Deakins (daunting critics, both), Deanna Dawson, Tim McCauley, Matthew McCauley, Brian Raper. I am particularly indebted to Leanne Jijian Hume for the moving cover photograph, to Beatrice Dowd, Tasha McCauley and Adrianna W. Van Leeuwen for painstaking editing and helpful suggestions, to Clive Pyne for the prototype index, and to Dawn-Louise McLeod for proof-reading.

The book's interior was designed by Fiona Raven; the cover and consolidating interior design elements are by Lawrence Boxall; final proofing was by Neall Calvert. The evidence of their skill is in your hands.

It is no exaggeration to register that *Making Sense of Us* might have remained either incomplete or forever in manuscript form if not for the very different modes of encouragement and practical help I have received, first from Deanna Dawson, Tim McCauley and Matthew McCauley, and subsequently from Jo Blackmore at Granville Island Publishing. If the ideas in the book eventually receive the wider consideration I hope for them, part of the credit will be owed in no small measure to those four very different fellow travelers. Great rivers come from many streams.

John Deakins

Index

abilities, conceptual/symbolic,
19–20, 31, 58, 67, 75–79, 106,
120–21, 151
abilities, perceptual and action,
5–7, 10, 17–18, 151
abilities, processing, 17–22, 27–
29
action. *See* abilities, perceptual
and action; action ambients
action ambients, 17, 18, 29–30,
58, 88–89, 100–101, 103, 119
activity
artistic, 59
conscious, 16
cooperative, 114
deceptive, 73, 91
inner, 33–34
instrumental and mental, 19,
20, 91, 96–99
and motive, 5
play, 58–59, 114
protective, 91, 93–94
affiliation(s), 48, 69, 109, 112–16,
128–30
affirmation(s), 56, 61, 91
agent, self as, 4–5, 56
See also God/gods
agent of change, 147–55

Alfie, 2, 133, 157–62
alienation, 109, 140, 143
aliveness, 3, 11, 15–16
ambients
definition, 16
See also action ambients;
conceptual ambients; human
ambients; institutional
ambients; perceptual
ambients; symbolic ambient
Animal Farm (Orwell), 147
anthropocentrism, 13, 74, 123,
162
Aristotle, 145–47
associative/dissociative
processes, 100, 102, 141, 145–
46, 158, 162–63
assumptions
and affiliations, 69, 113–14
associative/dissociative, 100
identity and beliefs, 48–55,
60–63, 105
instrumental symbol, 47–48, 68
about large questions, 2–7, 159–
61
about life, 45–47
and the nature of reality,
137–42

assumptions, institutional, 120, 123–24
assumptions, primary frame. *See* beliefs/assumptions, primary frame
Aung San Suu Kyi, 129
awareness
  beliefs, identity and, 40
  connected, 21–22, 26, 154, 160
  of the costs of change, 133–35, 137–38
  of incongruity, 100–101, 108, 152–54
  individuals and institutions, 126–27
  of the physical world, 43–44
  of self, 7–8, 13–14, 20–22, 157–60
  universal, 163–64
awareness, off centered
  absence of, 95
  vs. centric, 108, 139, 154–55, 172n5
  and curiosity, 51
  and deception, 78
  described, 21–23, 148, 150
  dialectic, 145–46
  history of, 81–82
  humane, 54
  in institutions, 117, 125–26
  the nature of costs, 135–36
  what it's all about, 157–59, 162–63

Baudelaire, Charles, 141, 182n4
behaviors, protective. *See* maneuvers, protective
being-in-the-world, 7, 31, 52, 121, 139–40, 154
belief, 33–44
  changing/questioning, 131–55

defending and protecting, xiii–xiv, 45
  extreme, 56
  and feedback, 52
  and identity, 105, 108
  openness to, 51–56
  propositional thought, 33–44
  and reality, 59–63
  status of, 97–98
  about value, 99–100
beliefs, fundamental. *See* beliefs/assumptions, primary frame
beliefs/assumptions, primary frame
  affiliations with others, 69
  and affirmations, 61–63
  and closed-mindedness
  cooperation and, 111–12, 116–17
  and effectiveness, 55–59, 123–24
  and identity, 105, 108–9
  imagined reality and, 59–63
  layered above, 50–54
  resistance to change/feedback, 49–51, 83–84, 142–43, 155
  scientific, 49–50
  skills and, 97–98
brain, reptilian, 92
Brecht, Bertolt, 150, 182n15
Bringhurst, Robert, 79
Bruner, Jerome, 54, 71
bureaucracy/bureaucratization. *See* institutions
Burke, Kenneth, xvi, 42–43, 79, 82–83, 141, 145, 164, 165, 166, 175n8, 179n5, 180n2, 184n18

camouflage, genetically-engineered, 73
Camus, Albert, 160, 184n1

Cassirer, Ernst, 165, 173n13, 174n9
centricity/centric
and change, 135–36
described, 21–23, 150
and early learning, 34, 54
and ecological balance, 172n6
humankind and, 154–55
and identity, 91–92
institutions, 127
as motivation, 139, 158–60
vs. off-centeredness, 95, 108, 135–36, 139, 150, 154–55, 172n5
and primary frame beliefs, 62–63, 108–9
change, 131–55
and beliefs, 131–55
costs of, 132–35, 137–38
distress and, 137–38
and effectiveness, 132–33
fear and hope, 131–32
and incongruity, 143–44, 150–54
potential agents of, 147–55
Chesterton, Gilbert Keith, 148–49
Cicero, 145
Climbing Mount Improbable (Dawkins), 5–6
closed-mindedness.
See open-mindedness/closed-mindedness
cognitions, emotional, 35–36
collusions, 103–5
communication, symbolic, 78, 88, 120
conceptual ambients, 19, 20–21, 27–31, 100–101, 102–3, 119, 173n13
conceptualization, 19–20, 26, 34, 36–37, 44, 67, 75–79

conflict, xiv, 63
connected awareness. *See* awareness, off-centered
consciousness, 10–11, 61, 91–92, 126, 145–46
continuity
of beliefs, 113, 123, 130
disruption in, 131–33, 136
of identity, 69, 90, 108–9, 115, 123
of meaning, 40–41, 48, 56, 61, 69, 97, 101, 106, 115, 129
cooperation, 111–30
communal affiliations, types of, 112–16
group (*See* institutions: and cooperation)
institutions, within, 116–30
potential for, 163
and purpose, 115, 116–17, 119
symbolic processes and, 26–27, 111–12, 120–21
creativity, 107
curiosity, 51, 52–53

Dawkins, Richard, 5–6
deception, 73, 75, 77–78
dehumanization, 57, 62–63, 121, 123
delusional schemes, 59–60
Dialogues (Plato), 143
differentiation, 25–26
discernment, 35–36, 78
discrimination, 8–9, 76, 87, 91–92
dissociative process. *See* associative/dissociative processes
distortions, 83–84, 102
dolphins, 13
Donne, John, 25–26, 137
doubt, 61

Douglas, Tommy, 63
Duncan, Isadora, 77

eccentricity. *See* centricity/centric
economizing procedures, 93–94
effectiveness, 42, 53, 55–60, 63,
    97, 132–33
Einstein, Albert, 37, 50, 78, 173n4
Ekman, Paul, 92–93
Elster, Jon, 95
empathy, 23–24, 172n8
engagement, terms of, 41
error(s), 65–84
    closed-mindedness and, 83
    and conceptualization, 67,
        75–78
    costs of, 42–43
    and familiar phenomenon,
        67–68
    freedom to, 82–83
    in judgment, 73–74
    the nature of, 63
    in perception, thinking and
        action, 65–84, 89–90, 102–3
    pre-conceptual learning and,
        71–72
    and survival, 65–67, 72
Essay on Man (Cassirer), 165,
    173n13
Essertier, Daniel, 61
evolution, conceptual, 28, 92,
    136–37, 163–64
evolution, of life, xii–xiii, 3–7,
    65–66, 92
experience
    and belief, 40–44
    and change, 138–40, 147–50
    direct and indirect, 9, 11–12, 28,
        34, 44, 45–47, 71–72, 85–87
    discrepant, 50–51, 53
    erroneous understandings, 67–
        68

and incongruity, 142–44
    openness to, 54–56
    of self and other, 108–9
    of the world, 14–16, 33–35
experience, symbolically
    mediated. *See* experience:
    direct and indirect

faith, 60–61, 161
feed-forward, 95–97
feedback
    correctness of, 42–44
    disconfirming, 52–53, 83–84
    learning from, 98–101
    openness to, 133, 139–40
    within organizations, 122–27,
        129–30
    suppressing, 93, 117
    vulnerability to, 45–46
feeling-states, 23–25
feelings, 35, 36, 38–39, 102–3,
    131, 166
Feyerabend, Paul, 161, 184n3
final cause. *See* God/gods
Flanders, Michael, 34, 36
Franklin, Ursula, 79
Freire, Paulo, 153–54, 184n18
Friesen, Wallace, 92–93
Frye, Herman Northrop, 145–47
Function of Reason, The
    (Whitehead), 165–66
functions, 6–19, 38, 119, 126–27
fundamental beliefs/
    assumptions. *See* beliefs/
    assumptions, primary frame

genes/genetics, 10, 28, 33, 65–66,
    72–73
God/gods, 4–5, 50, 60, 78, 81–82,
    103, 160–62, 178
Goffman, Erving, 48–49, 174n9
Grene, Marjorie, 21, 172n5

group. *See* institutions
Gusfield, Joseph R., 166

habit, 93
Hamlet (Shakespeare), 39
Hawking, Stephen, 103, 180n10
Henle, Paul, 167
Hitler, Adolf, 145
Hoban, Russell, 31
hostility, 56–57
human ambients, 17–31
  centricity and off-centeredness,
    21–23
  conceptualize, ability to, 19–21
  constituents of, 30
  and empathy, 23–24
  range and limitations of, 17–19,
    58, 82–83, 113, 120
  reality, ideas about, 27–31
human rights, 129
humankind, 26, 29, 57, 81–83, 90,
  136–37, 154, 160, 171n12
hypotheses, 36, 51

identity, 91–109
  and belief, 40, 145–46
  deception and, 106–8
  and feedback, 98–99, 100–101
  group, 61
  institutional, 69, 117–19,
    121–23
  about interests, self and other,
    94–95
  loss of, 133
  merged, 25–26
  protecting, 45, 56, 91–95,
    100–105, 108–9
  and relationships, 91, 104–5
  sense of self and, 41, 48–50, 148
  survival and, 45, 68
  threat to, 84

image. *See* beliefs/assumptions,
  primary frame
incongruity
  our own, 150
  anticipation and reality, 66–67
  appraising, 88–89
  and beliefs, 49
  costs of, 135
  the critical mode, 52–53
  encountering an, 151–54
  in experience, 143–44
  and feedback, 83–84, 100–101
  suppressing awareness of, 108
inner world, 15
instincts, 29, 33, 45, 65–66
institutional ambients, 118–20,
  126
institutions
  and change, 131, 136
  constituents of, 119
  and cooperation, 111–30
  and feedback, 83, 124–26,
    129–30
  and identity, 69, 121–23
  individuals within, 117–18,
    120–23, 126–30
  protective procedures, 123–26,
    129
  purpose, 111–17, 119, 120–23,
    126–27
intelligence, human, 20, 29,
  145–46, 173n15

judgment, errors in, 73–74
junk-terms, 67–68, 76

Kaplan, Abraham, 67, 78–79, 94
Kraus, Elizabeth M., 166

La Fontaine, Jean de, 85, 179n1

Langer, Susanne K., 20, 23, 24, 31,
 36, 61, 81, 111, 165, 166,
 170n6, 172n7, 174n9, 178n24,
 179n1
language, 3, 19, 33–35, 39–40,
 46–47, 53–54, 76
Lao Tse, 180n4
Lasker, Emanuel, 94
laughter, 150
law of the instrument, 78–79
learning
 conceptual and pre-conceptual,
 34, 66–67, 71–72
 cumulative, 65–67
 direct and indirect, 46–47
 early, 43–44, 54
 and feedback, 98–101
 later life, 55
 practical and emotional, 43–44
L'Étranger (Camus), 160
lies, 44
life, making sense of, xiv–xvii,
 13–16, 34–35, 41–42, 157–64
life-space, 40–41
loss, 132–33
Lovelock, James, 13, 101, 171n14
Lowen, Alexander, 92–93
Lynch, Kevin, 8, 40–41

making sense. *See* life, making
 sense of
maneuvers, protective, 49, 63,
 93–94, 100–101, 103, 105,
 108–9, 124–25
Margulis, Lynn, 171n14
Maruyama, Magorah, 67
Mau-Mauing the Flak-Catchers
 (Wolfe), 124
McClean, Paul, 92
McKay, D.M., 95–96
meaning
 of an act, 95
 204

centric, 22
 of conceptualizations, 33–34, 75
 distorted, 102
 existence, of our own, 136–37
 of experiences, 50–51, 93
 of feedback, 44
 in language, 46
 subjective, 55–56
 symbolic, 38, 77–78, 127
 See also continuity: of
 meaning
measures, protective. *See*
 maneuvers, protective
mental representation. *See*
 symbolic representation:
 mental
metaphor, xv–xvi, 7, 79–80, 85,
 123
Metaphysics of Experience, The
 (Krauss), 166
mind, 31, 33, 163
 See also open-mindedness/
 closed-mindedness
*Mind: An Essay on Human
 Feeling* (Langer), 166
misrepresentation, 27, 154
Modes of Thought (Whitehead),
 165–66
morality, 53–54, 77, 129, 162–63
motivation
 attribution of, 81–82
 centric, 100, 108
 to change, 131–55
 deceptive, 78
 determinants of, 59–60, 67–68
 human, 17–18, 98–99
 a major element, 38–39
 of others, 56–57
 permeated with, 3–5
 and responsibility, 107
 risk *vs.* advantage, 106
 and survival, 45, 62–63

See also purpose

Nature, xii, 3, 12–13, 16, 78, 163, 171n14
1984 (Orwell), 147
Northrop, F.S.C., 167
Nuremberg Principles, 129

objective. *See* purpose
objectivity, 21
off-centeredness. *See* awareness, off-centered
On Symbols and Society (Gusfield), 166
Onley, Toni, 182–83n16
open mindedness/closed-mindedness, ix, 50–55, 83, 135
opportunity, optimizing, 85–90
opportunity, survival and, 45–63
organizations. *See* institutions
Orwell, George, 144–45, 147
outer world concept, 15–16
See also ambients

perception. *See* abilities, perceptual and action; perceptual ambients
perceptual ambients, 17–18, 29, 30, 58, 86–88, 100–102, 119, 172n2
Permanence and Change (Burke), 166
perspective, x–xi, 121, 148–50
persuasion, 95–96, 145–46
Philosophy in a New Key (Langer), 166
Philosophy of Symbolic Forms, The (Cassirer), 165, 173n13
Picasso, Pablo, 77
Plato, 143
play, 58–59
Plessner. Helmuth, 21

polarization, 60–63, 146–47, 182n4
Pollak, Otto, 25
primary frame beliefs/assumptions. *See* beliefs/assumptions, primary frame
Principia Mathematica (Whitehead and Russell), 54
procedures, economizing, 93
Process and Reality, An Essay in Cosmology (Whitehead), 165–66
processes abilities (*See* abilities, processing)
associative/dissociative (*See* associative/dissociative processes)
of bureaucratization, 117
cooperation and beliefs about, 114, 116–17, 122–23
essential, 5–16
evolutionary, 65–66, 136, 158–59, 163–64
feedback (*See* feedback)
of making sense, xii
propositions about, 38
symbolic, 27–31, 56–63, 111
the world as, 99–100
projection, 102–3, 107, 140, 148
propositional form, 34
propositional structure, 39–40
propositional thought, 33–37, 44, 65
propositions about beliefs/assumptions, 41–43, 45–46, 99, 144
about error, 75–76, 83
about experience, 102–4
general form of, 49
about identity, 40–41

predetermining, 157
types of, 37–39
public relations, 124–26
purpose, 1–5, 20, 41, 160–62
purpose, author's, xiv–xvi
Pye, David, 19

reality
collective, 27
faulty assumptions about,
137–55
imagined, 59–60
of institutions, 122
nature of, 36, 136–37
orders of, 37–39
physical, 136–37, 142
spurious, 83–84
subjective, of self, 157–58
sum of beliefs, 41–42
understanding the, 162
relationships. *See* affiliation(s)
religion, 61–63
See also God/gods
representational systems. *See*
symbolic representation
responsibility, 105–7, 136–37,
138, 140
rhetoric, 145–47
Rubinstein, Arthur, 97
Russell, Bertrand, 54

Sacks, Oliver, 184n2
security, emotional and physical,
52–53, 54
self-consciousness, 20–21
senses, world experienced by the.
See perceptual ambients
sharks in the mind, 31
Shaw, George Bernard, 141, 144,
147, 149
Shelley, Percy Bysshe, 150

Shklovsky, Viktor, 151, 182–
83n16
shock tactics, 141–44
significance, 74, 82
skills, cognitive and executive,
95–99
Spinoza, Baruch, 12
Stalker Affair, The (Stalker), 180–
81n5
Steiner, Claude, 104
stimulus-response theory, 71
Stravinsky, Igor, 87
supreme agent. *See* God/gods
survival, of species, xiii–xiv, 5–16,
43, 45–63, 65–66
Swann, Donald, 34, 36
symbolic ambient, 88–89, 173n13
symbolic communication, 120
symbolic forms, 20–21, 80–81,
165–66, 173n13
symbolic processes. *See* symbolic
representations
symbolic representations
characteristics of, 19–23
a complex mix, 72–83
and conceptualization, 19–23,
36–37
and danger, 92–93
effective and/or delusional, 58
63
and emotional learning, 35,
46–48
and feedback, 43–44
and institutions, 118–20,
123–24
and language, 35–36
mental, 18, 27–30, 33, 79–80
potential of, 158–59
two-faced, 70–71
See also skills, cognitive and
executive

symbolic rewards/approval,
    127–28
*Symbolism: Its Meaning and
    Effect* (Whitehead), 165–66
sympathy, 23–24, 62, 150
synthetic extensions, 19

terms and tools, 79–80
terms of engagement, 41
theatre, 24, 144
threat
  to being, 57
  to beliefs, 45, 49–51, 84
  of doubt, 61
  to identity, 40–41, 49–50, 84,
    91–109
  to institutions, 123–25, 129–30
  to sense of self, 53
Tolstoi, Leo, 151
truth, 77–78, 145–47

uncertainty and ambivalence, 81,
    105, 107, 132, 162

value, 38–39, 63, 99, 128–29
Vanishing Face of Gaia, The
    (Lovelock), 13, 101
victimization, 104–5
violence, 63
Von Uexküll, Jakob, 15–16, 27,
    86–87
  See also ambients

Watergate, 69
Westray mine disaster, 129–30
"What's it all about?", 1–16,
    157–58
Whitehead, Alfred North, 37, 51,
    54, 78, 165–66, 175–76n11
Williams, William Carlos, 59
Wittgenstein, Ludwig, 49, 50
Wolfe, Tom, 124

About the Author

JOHN DEAKINS was trained as a social worker at the University of Bristol in England, and at the University of Chicago in the United States.

In England he was initially involved in the rehabilitation of refugees expelled from Egypt at the time of the 1956 Suez war, and then worked for three years with the East London Family Service Unit, an agency working intensively with multiple-problem families.

In the United States he worked for six years with clients of the Jewish Family and Community Services in different locations in Chicago. His clients have primarily been families struggling to deal with both external pressures and internal crises, but he has also worked with the mentally ill, juvenile offenders, disturbed and physically injured children, and survivors of the holocaust.

He and his family moved to Canada in 1969, and for more than twenty years he was involved in training and overseeing the supervision of students in undergraduate and graduate programs of social work at the University of British Columbia. He received his Ph.D. from the School of Social Service Administration, the University of Chicago in 1972. He lives in Vancouver, British Columbia.